When Women Pray

How to Rekindle Your Faith for Greater Exploits in Christ

Jaime M Kang, PhD

professional before attempting any techniques outlined in this book.

By reading this document, the reader agrees that under no circumstances is the author responsible for any losses, direct or indirect, that are incurred as a result of the use of the information contained within this document, including, but not limited to, errors, omissions, or inaccuracies.

Unless otherwise noted, Scripture quotations are from *The NKJV Study Bible, Second Edition*, the New King James Version.

Table Of Contents

To my children,
Andrew, Cheryl, Benny, and Becca

&

To my grandchildren,
Lucas, Lynnette, and Nathaniel

FORWARD

Being a Christian remains one of the greatest gifts anyone can have, but being a Christian woman comes with a different level of grace and elegance. Women, all over the world, are recognized as the pillars of development, beacons of human empathy, and the foundation of the multiplicity of mankind. However, in Christendom, we recognize women, not just with the aforementioned qualities, but also as the cradle of the salvation of the world.

When you look around, from the east to the west, and from the north to the south, the success of societies is often attributed to the steadfastness of women who either stood by their men or did one thing or the other to save their societies. Though seemingly physically weaker than men, it has been proven that women have successfully undergone the pangs of childbirth, the pain only women can experience. There is something special about being a woman; this special feature finds expression in how women act, how we relate with others and with God.

I consider it an honor to be born a woman, and a greater

honor to be a Christian woman. The reason for this is not difficult to understand, it lies in the major roles that women play in the lives of others. There is an analogy that describes women as the 'neck' while men are the head. The moment you cut off the neck, the head loses base and profoundly becomes useless.

However, many women still wallow in ignorance, wasting their time and their lives in an unworthy cause. Our world is filled with thousands of women who have lost sight of what it means to be a woman and to be in Christ Jesus. I understand that society socializes women to reduce themselves, to be less ambitious, and to conceal themselves behind the cloak of submission. Yet, we find that when Christ came, he paid attention to women than never before. He challenged the status quo of subsuming women, shaming, or denigrating them.

A little walk into the past, when a woman was accused of adultery in the gospel of John 8:3, the scribes and the Pharisees had said she is due for death by stoning. We notice the subtle approach Jesus employed in dismissing them: *so when they continued asking Him, He raised Himself up and said, "He who is without sin among you, let him throw a stone at her first" (John 8:7).* But that wasn't a case for me, I am amazed at how they brought the woman without bringing the man with whom she committed the offence; that shows that women had always been victims of certain laws, including the Jewish laws. Jesus was able to save this condemned adulteress, and what he did was beyond saving this woman. He gave women the boldness to step out their sins, come to him and be forgiven.

Jesus has shown that it isn't a world of men, but a world of both genders. He has torn down the societal veil of *always-hide-yourself* to a new and loving garment of *you're-equally-important-powerful-and-appreciated.*

This book is all about the place as women and how we can maximize our God-given positions of authority, power, and influence. There is need to get more women to see how they can perform deeper exploits in Christ through prayers and faith. When women pray, it does mighty things, it opens up the heavens in a different way, and it causes God to pour down his dews of kindness. Imagine what the fate of the bridegroom would have been if Mary did not attend the wedding at Cana of Galilee (John 2). Or, what if Mary decided to sit back like every other guest and watch events unfold?

The Bible records that she had compassion, and she approached Jesus, telling Him that wine had finished. John, the beloved, recorded that *when they ran out of wine, the mother of Jesus said to Him, "They have no wine" (John 2:3).* Notice that Mary did not just intercede on behalf of the celebrants; she influenced Jesus to work miracles before the appointed time. Jesus had retorted in verse 4 of the same chapter, *"Woman, what does your concern has to do with me? My hour has not yet come."* Mary did not give up, she knew she could not be turned down by her own son, especially when her request was aligned to Jesus's mission to help the poor. Oh, I can imagine the expression on the face of the bridegroom when wine *came out of nowhere!* He must have felt elated, salvaged, and revived; all because a woman decided to step into the situation.

Now, two things came into play in this scenario. One is empathy – the ability to share in the burden of another. Mary was obviously empathetic and didn't want the groom to face the impending shame. This is very common among women; we are naturally emotional, and this is further fine-tuned when a woman is in Christ. Now, this leads to the second point of the Canaan wedding: Swift action! Mary knew there was a problem, and she needed to do something. She thought fast, and she came up with an ever-wonderful solution.

The Christian woman is a woman of power, she has authority in Christ, beyond what she knows. *When Women Pray* comes as an eye-opener to how far a woman can go in life and ministry. It begins by exploring the place of women, the relevance of womanhood, showing how the world is utterly incomplete without women. The book then goes ahead to define prayer and faith in relative to the woman in Christ. You'll soon discover how prayer works, and the way you can pray better, utilizing the instruments of faith and persistence.

Furthermore, you'll also learn about the things that prevent women from taking their place, both self-inflicted and society-imposed factors. Like expected, the book shows you how to overcome these impediments and get yourself going.

Every chapter ends with a sincere prayer and a Bible study guide to ensure a deeper connection with the teachings. It promises to be a good read, scripture-based, inspiring, and life-changing.

1

Women Make the World Complete

The sun had already set, and it was gradually getting dark; still in my office, I was scrolling through the pages of a new eBook I've just purchased from Amazon. Deeply engrossed in this inspiring book of church history; recounting the faith of the early church, the communal life, and the entire beautiful rapport that existed among people in the early church. I heard a knock on the door, it was quite unexpected; no one had told me they'd be visiting me after my office hours. You know this feeling of being distracted from a very important program…and I reluctantly went for the door.

Sunnie, one of my students, stood by the door, transfixed, crestfallen; and the moment our eyes met, she burst into tears. One would easily think she lost a loved one, was robbed or may have landed into some serious trouble. I gently held her hand, lead her into the house, and helped her to sit down.

We sat very close to each other, and all I could deduce from her sobs was a deeply broken heart. So, we got talking, she narrated her ordeal with a classmate.

She got into an argument with this classmate who went off to the point of contention to tell her that she was a woman who didn't have what it takes to speak to him, she was a mere lady who does not matter anywhere except in the childbirth, and other demeaning words based on her gender. She felt terrible and dehumanized, the young man who was known to be a strong Christian, had made her appear as though it was a crime to be a woman. I could feel the anger in her heart, the feeling of being worthless, not necessarily because you are unproductive, but because you are a woman.

That is the kind of society we live in, a world that easily discounts the action of women, but hastily defends the same action when it is taken by a man. I didn't know exactly how to console my student, Sunnie; we're all used to the popular chants like: women matter too, women are powerful, women are great and industrious, whatever a man can do, a woman can do even better! These are generic stuff that we hear every day, not only feminists scream them, but other women say them, too.

However, the Holy Spirit has a way of speaking to us when we do not know what to say, and I am quickly reminded of the words of Jesus while he was admonishing the apostles, he said, *...do not worry about how or what you should speak.*

For it will be given to you in that hour what you should speak (Matthew 10:19). I took a deep breath, and then I asked her a question, do you know that the world is incomplete without women? She looked a bit perplexed. I held her hands, looking directly into her eyes, and I said: the world would have been messy, uninhabitable, and incomplete without you. She wasn't the first person I said those words to, but like most women, it always sounded absurd until we went deeper. We've all been socialized to count ourselves 'second class' citizens of the world, people who must always operate from the background. We have a culture that teaches women to keep quiet even when it is not comfortable to keep quiet, so it always sounds like folktale when you tell a woman that the world is incomplete without her.

In this chapter, I'll take you to the Bible to show how important the female gender is to the world, especially among Christians. The intention is not to blow our own trumpets or to showcase some narcissistic, gender-inspired piece of advertisement. The idea is to reestablish the fact that women can, and, in fact, are useful. It doesn't matter what the world thinks or what the socializations are; what matters is that there is a position specially crafted by God to be occupied by the female folks. Any attempt to undermine this position will always result in disorder, and as we know it, when there is no order, we can never move forward.

Adam without Eve

The first thing I told Sunnie was the story of creation. It's a story we're all familiar with, it doesn't do any good reproducing here. But have you imagined what the life of Adam was until Eve was created? The Bible recounts that God created animals of all kinds and colors; trees of various heights and shapes; beautiful flowers, and other vegetables orderly placed around the Garden of Eden. As a matter of truth, God looked at what He had made, and saw they were good (Genesis 1:31). God discovers that His creation is really good and wonderful, but, all of a sudden, He felt something was lacking. Just imagine that you were preparing a pot of soup, you added all ingredients, it looks so lip-smacking and sumptuous, but just when you thought you'd made the best soup, you discover you didn't add salt!

That was exactly how God felt when He discovered the absence of a woman in the creation narrative. Just like all the other creatures, the man needed someone to attend to him. God made a woman and covered up the gap quickly. God, in His infinite wisdom, knew that a woman can successfully complete His work of creation.

The implication is that if God didn't make a woman, Adam would not just be lonely, he would disappear without a trace. Remember he was made out of clay, his body cannot just last forever, it doesn't matter how we choose to view it. The Bible was clear that man was made out of dirt, he meant nothing and was nothing until God breathed into him, giving him a spirit unto His likeness. Genesis 2:7 reports it thus: *And God formed man of the dust of the ground, and breathed into his nostrils the breath of life; and man became a living being.* It simply means that man's body would still get old, even if he didn't sin.

Upon the creation of a woman, we notice the instant fulfillment of God's instruction to increase and multiply. A man couldn't have pulled this through if a woman wasn't created. I can imagine the joy on Adam's face when his first child was born, the joy in heaven when God's instruction to multiply was kept.

In all these, it is pertinent to understand that God, who is all-knowing, has given women a highly exalted position. The complexity of a woman's body is far-reaching compared to that of a man, she performs functions that only she can perform.

By the time I'd finished explaining this to Sunnie, I could notice the relief that came with the exposition; it isn't like this story is new, it's just that we need to see it from a different perspective that places women in the limelight.

We should begin to understand that the creation of a woman wasn't a happenstance, it was completely intentional. Let's take it a little further by exploring the salvation of the world through Christ.

It is already established that our God is a God of order, who doesn't like to overlook the process. He knew a time will come when a savior will be born. The prophet Isaiah had predicted that a child will be born through a virgin: *Behold, the virgin shall conceive and bear a son, and shall His name Immanuel (Isaiah 7:14).*

Many years after this prophecy, God fulfilled them through the birth of Jesus. What could have been the fate of humanity if God didn't create a woman who would carry the savior of the world for nine months until delivery? That shows that no matter how much we toss around, everything about the balance of people in the world, the continued existence of humans, and the new life we now enjoy in Christ, are all linked to women. Notice that God bypassed the man, and Mary got pregnant without the carnal knowledge of Joseph, she was overwhelmed by the Holy Spirit. But the place of the woman couldn't be bypassed, it must be followed strictly.

As a measure of grace and value placed upon women, when Zechariah questioned the angel, Gabriel, he instantly became deaf and dumb till John was born (Luke 1:11-20). Mary committed the same offence, she asked: *How can this be, since I do not know a man? (Luke 1:34).* Instead of the normal Zechariah-treatment, the Bible recorded that the angel of God took time to explain to Mary, breaking down the details of her assignment. She was important, even God didn't want to take chances. Again, God doesn't infringe on people's right, he needed Mary to be aware, and, perhaps, consent to the plan. Mary did accept God's proposal by saying in Luke 1:38, *Behold the maidservant of the Lord! Let it be to me according to your word.* Now, that may sound a bit like over-flogging the importance of women, but it really isn't. After all, it is never wrong to claim what is rightly yours.

Many women face suggestions in their everyday life experiences that they are less important or valued. It is never true. You, as a woman, is the most important of everything you can think of. Nothing ever works unless women are partly or completely involved.

The Ministry of Womanhood

While I was reflecting, one morning, on what it means to be a woman, I felt the need to quickly dismantle any negative thought that might get hold of your mind. Maybe the words above are beginning to sound like women are superior, or more important than men. What we tried to establish in the previous section wasn't a theory of women's superiority over men, no! It was simply an honest evaluation of how important we are as women.

The Bible was very clear in explaining that there are roles meant for each gender, no gender is practically superior, one performs their role to complement the other. We do not belong to the same ship with people who believe in jealousy or unnecessary competition between the two genders, our message is that of *'complementalism'*. We all know that the initial plan of God was to make the man a helper, a companion; in this same way, women help men, and men help women. We do not compete. The woman knows her roles as a daughter, a mother, a wife, etc.

That the ministry of womanhood is somehow relegated to the background has profound importance. I was going through a text by an unknown author, and she was trying to emphasize the fact that womanhood goes beyond the biological configuration. It is something that finds expression in how we walk, work, speak, relate, help, etc. Though her text was more like a feminist-motivational-piece, I was interested in the fact that womanhood goes beyond our biological configuration.

There is a huge difference between someone who was born a woman, and someone who acquired the female characteristics artificially. The womanhood is a divine ministry, ordained by God to offer certain services to humanity.

Beginning from the family where she helps a man to stand, nurtures children, her work goes into the church where she fits into *any* position, preacher, teacher, prophet, steward, among others. A woman can as well, comfortably support the administration of any society unto any level. Being a helper doesn't mean she is always supposed to be in less-important positions, it means she has the capacity to build further than what the man has done. Invariably, a man can move from point A to point B, then with the assistance of a woman, he moves further to point C.

This is the basis of almost all the remaining parts of the book: how to rekindle your faith for deeper exploits in Christ. Your faith, which is supposed to be built on God, is not just meant to be redundant. Your womanhood entails that you help. The help, in this regard, is not limited to helping a spouse; the help that women offer is broad, it encompasses all human endeavors, from helping yourself, through helping others, and to helping the society. It is quite erroneous to narrowly define a *helper* as someone who never stands out, or someone who should never be seen. It is too limited to fit into God's agenda for the women.

Womanhood means that you appreciate your femininity, you're proud of who you are. It means you're comfortable with being a helper. To be a woman means to offer love, care, empathy, and emotional support. When we explore the nature of a woman, we understand that we naturally get easily emotional than men, it isn't a coincidence, it is part of God's big plan. Even when Jesus was being dragged to Golgotha for His crucifixion, the Bible recorded that women wept and cried behind him.

It wasn't like there were no men who supported Christ through His journey to the cross, but the physical presence of the women meant a lot. Imagine when Christ had fallen the second time, looking all around and he neither sees his apostles nor any of his followers, He will definitely feel devastated. In essence, the ministry of womanhood is one that stands by the weak, the poor, and the oppressed.

A woman is subtle by nature. The implication of this is that a woman can step into corners where a man will be pushed away, she can walk into places and situations where her male counterparts will fail. This is what the ministry of womanhood is capable of doing if properly utilized. Let me remind you of the life of Mother Teresa as an example.

As the famous story goes, Mother Teresa was greatly influenced by the humane treatment her mother provided for people; going by her mother's footsteps, she dedicated her life to serving indigent people around the world. She commanded a special kind of influence than any world leader could have garnered. It is reported that in the last phase of her missions, she never paid for a flight, and for every flight she joins, people contributed generously immediately they discover that she was aboard.

Mother Teresa, whose footprints will ever remain upon the surface of the earth, is a vivid example of maximizing the ministry of womanhood. The affection and flair for caring come with every woman; we don't learn it, it's part of who we are.

Womanhood is never a competition for power; rather, it is a quest for a better, safer society. That was the exact reason for our creation – to complete what was once hollow, give it shape, and help it to expand.

I disparage the thinking, especially as paraded by modern feminism, that women should be given a certain level of high-handedness or slapdash equality with men. I heard a hardcore feminist preaching that when a woman gives birth to a child, her husband can also get *paternity leave*, to care for the child while the woman continues with her work. Their demand is predicated on the fact that the child is equally owned by the man and the woman, the burden of childcare should not be left on the shoulders of women alone. There is, of course, an element of sensibility in this claim; but it is time we understand that a child comes from a woman's body, the child got used to your body even before birth. In the case of breastfeeding a child for instance, how will the father of the child cope? These are pointers to the fact that childcare is not an exclusively reserved job for the woman, but she's best fitted for it.

The ministry of womanhood is not a ministry of competition, it is a ministry that seeks, helps, improves, and is to complement

Standing Your Ground as a Christian Woman

In October 2016, I had the opportunity of speaking to a group of young women. It was more or less like a conference that had participants from different parts of the country;

they were all quite expectant, hoping to leave the venue with something tangible.

When it was my turn to speak, I mounted the podium and delivered a sermon on a topic called *Let the Changed People Change the World*. It was quite a fulfilling moment for myself and my audience, the spirit of the Lord was able to arrest every soul, gently ministering to us.

At the end of the program, a young lady walked up to me, she said she wanted to ask me some personal questions that were troubling her. "I've been born-again for a while now, I love God, and I love the things of God; but I've noticed that the pressures keep on increasing daily. I am faced with a lot of pressures, some directly, others indirectly…" I didn't wait for her to finish because I already know where she's headed. She is in a society that keeps defining paths for women against their wish, a culture where women transform their bodies in various ways to fit into the society's definition of beauty and excellence. It is increasingly becoming difficult for a Christian woman to say no to most of these things, you are made to appear awkward, foolish, and unintelligent.

We find women, even Christian women who get plastic surgery to enhance their looks and endowments. Those things are not inherently wrong; in fact, it is good to look good. What matters most is our intention. In Proverbs 21:2, the scriptures say *we can justify every of our actions, but God looks at the motive.* Put in another way, *every way of a man is right in his own eyes, but the Lord weighs the hearts.*

What is your motive for enhancing your looks? To look good for yourself, or to show off your wealth? Or out of jealousy or fear of losing someone you love? If our motive for taking actions are aligned with the heartbeat of the Holy Spirit, then there is no problem.

Paul was counseling the Corinthians, and he said, *do not be unequally yoked together with unbelievers. For what fellowship has righteousness with lawlessness? And what communion has light with darkness (2 Corinthians 6:14)?* This admonition which was meant for the entire body of Christ has a special place in the lives of women.

Women are more vulnerable to pressure. We're most likely to adapt to changes than our male counterparts, so modern culture is a factor we should be cautious of. I've cited an example above, but that is not the only phenomenon we battle as women. We're faced with a myriad of them. In all these, we are called to be steadfast, trusting in God to keep us safe, and help us to maintain our grounds as Christians, and as women.

In any case, we must still put in complete and conscious efforts towards sustaining ourselves; this can be done in a number of ways which we will discuss in full in subsequent chapters. The most important, however, remains that we should take care not to immerse ourselves in things that do not matter. One of the major ways we get ourselves into the trouble of loosing-our-values is through the kind of people we mingle with, the kind of literature we read, and the ones we see with our eyes. If a Christian woman, for instance, wants to avoid the pressures of the world, yet she continues to read amoral magazines, surfing unholy sites, mingling freely with unbelievers, her quest to protect her faith will surely amount to nothing.

Finally, this whole chapter was dedicated to preparing your mind and setting it aright for the task ahead. The sole aim is to help you understand and appreciate womanhood. This will foster a better understanding of your place in Christ, as you take a deeper walk into the ancient wisdom of the Most High.

Prayer

Eternal Father, whose intention was to make me a helper to the whole of humanity, help me to understand my place as a woman. Open the eyes of my understanding, and enable me to know that I am equally important as any other person in the world, I am dearly valued, and I am precious to Christ. Grant that I may perform my duties without competing with men; save me, dear Lord, from modern teachings and heresies. Help me to be a woman, help me to be a Christian woman. Amen.

A Glance through Your Bible

Genesis 1:26-28, 2:18

^{1:26}Then God said, "Let us make man in our image, according to our likeness; let them have dominion over the fish of the sea, over the birds of the air, and over the cattle, over all the earth and over every creeping thing that creeps on the earth." ²⁷So God created man in His own image; in the image of God He created them; male and female he created them. ²⁸Then God blessed them, and God said to them, "Be fruitful and multiply; fill the earth and subdue it; have dominion over the fish of the sea, over the birds of the air, and over every living thing that moves on the earth." . . .

^{2:18} And the Lord God said, "It is not good that a man should be alone; I will make him a helper comparable to him.

Study Questions

- Does the Bible suggest in any way, that women are inferior?

- What does it mean to be a helper?

- Are you truly a Christian woman? If yes, what makes you a Christian woman?

- If your answer was no, what are the things you need to change? Write them out.

- Do you believe in the ministry of womanhood? Why?

- Is any gender, male/female, superior to the other?

- What does the Bible say about your relationship with unbelievers?

2

Defining Faith and Prayer

Faith is deliberate confidence in the character of God whose ways you may not understand at the time. – Oswald Chambers

Eugene, a friend of mine from college, loves basketball. In our college years, he played for a local basketball team, a social team of passionate young men like him. Though I hadn't much interest in basketball, and indeed, any contact sports, but my friendship with Eugene made me develop a little interest. He would often tell me about his teammates and their individual characters, how they plan to defeat another team with a large margin. Once Eugene begins a conversation about his team, their training, the winnings, and the few defeats, I notice a tinge of confidence in his voice and mannerism. Eugene demonstrates so well that you'll begin to feel like you were there. On one of those days, ahead of a match they'd play the same day, I asked him what he thought the outcome of the match would be; without mincing words, he said that the team they were going to face was nothing compared to his. "We'll beat them, hands down!" he boasted.

Well, it wasn't the first time he talked about beating another team, and upon my enquiry, he said his team trains better than any other. They have the best players, and that he *had faith* in what they could do. I took it down in my notepad, knowing that I may need it someday. By the time I revisited it many years later, I began to ask myself certain questions. Why was Eugene so confident? Why were members of his team confident too? Has their confidence anything to do with their winnings, and trophies?

Answers to these questions may not seem too easy, but they are quite simple and can be figured out quickly. By the time I began to study about faith, I discovered that Eugene didn't just brag, he *had faith* in his team. The truth about his faith is that he believed that they train very well, the training (proper training), was the prerequisite for having the upper hand over your opponent. But it doesn't end at that; training also helped them to build confidence, knowing that they have what it takes to win a match.

If Eugene exercised such kind of faith/confidence in his teammates and the kind of training they received, why will I ever need to faint as a Christian, or as a Christian woman? In due course, I began an exploration into this concept of faith, and what it is all about. I discovered that it is like the battery that sustains us as Christians. The entirety of Christianity is built on faith in an unseen God; none of us has ever seen God, yet we believe so strongly that there is a God who watches over the affairs of men. As though believing in God isn't enough, we also believe that Christ left His throne in heaven, came to earth as a man – in flesh and blood, was crucified, died, and was buried. We didn't have a first-hand experience of these things, yet we believe they happened. We didn't all witness His ascension, but we believe He did ascend to heaven.

In all these, we believe what we were told about Christ, we believe, we honor, and we trust that He'll come someday to take the saints; but something is missing. I noticed that we tend to believe more in the existence of God, but we do not have a strong belief in the power of His might. This is not meant to confuse you in any way, I am simply saying that it is one thing to know that God exists and that He is in heaven watching over us, but it is another thing to truly believe that He has the ability to change situations, and cause things to favor us. That is where true faith comes in. The Bible is laden with a lot of promises made by God to man. There are pieces of evidence that He's a God who keeps His words, yet, something about our time and age has made us feel indifferent about trusting God and in the power of His might.

Many people appear in church, fellowshipping with other brethren, but they still nurse ill-feelings about God. They are not sure if they'll eventually get anything good from serving God. We can simply describe them as people who are part of the body of Christ because they want to have some feeling of belonging; there is no real connection to the mysteries of God, the story of the cross, and the hope of redemption. Though we are faced with many circumstances, it never suggests that God caused them, or that He isn't aware of what's happening. Perhaps, we haven't just done what we're supposed to do. And that is where faith and prayer come in.

Have you ever thought of what God meant when He said in Numbers 14:28, *"As I live," says the Lord, "just as you have spoken in My hearing, so I will do to you."* It means that God is actually waiting to hear from you, but you've refused to speak. Away from this direct instruction, God had also spoken through Paul, and He said, *Be anxious for nothing, but in everything by prayer and supplication, with thanksgiving, let your requests be made known to God (Philippians 4:6).* The problem is that we always expect God to step into the situation without inviting Him. However, He is not a God that 'invades privacy.' He is patiently waiting for you to make your requests known. Instead of making your requests known to God, you keep on lamenting and narrating your ordeals to people who cannot help you.

In this chapter, we're concerned about knowing what faith is.

We shall explore the connection between faith and prayer. We shall also take a closer look at the kind of prayer that works, and commands results. It is my desire that at the end of this chapter, your faith must have been raised to a level where you can say effective prayers and receive answers from God.

What Is Faith?

Among the Catholic faithful, there is a definition of faith they often recite, and I find it useful to note here: *Faith is the supernatural gift of God, which enables us to believe without doubt, whatever God has revealed.* If we pick this definition to pieces, the first important thing is that we believe **without** doubt. To believe without doubt is synonymous to saying, "God said it! Any other thing can come behind." This Catholic definition of faith, I think, captures the reality of what it means to have faith in God. Now, we take a walk through the scriptures, and we find a woman named Sarah; the Bible records that she was way past the age of childbirth. In modern times, we're told that a woman reaches menopause at the age of 45. In the case of Sarah, there was a quick alteration of this scientific limitation, and in Hebrews 11:11, the scriptures say: *And by faith even Sarah, who was past childbearing age, was enabled to bear children because she considered Him faithful who had made the promise.*

Sarah knew she was old, and naturally, she cannot bear a child. Her husband, Abraham, was also old, they both no longer have what it takes to bear a child. *So Sarah laughed to herself as she thought, "After I am worn out and my lord is old, will I now have this pleasure?" (Genesis 18:12).* Yet, there is a God who has promised to give them a son. In Genesis 17:16, the Lord spoke to Abraham, and He said, *I will bless her and will surely give you a son by her. I will bless her so that she will be the mother of nations; kings of peoples will come from her.* God continues to promise Abraham and Sarah of a son, of being parents of many nations. It is further expressed in Genesis 18:10 ...I *will surely return to you about this time next year, and Sarah your wife will have a son.*

Amidst these things, Sarah looked beyond her weak body and the old age of her husband. She was only interested in the fact that the Lord had revealed, and so she believed without doubt.

Has God Revealed It?

This is a critical question to the exercise of faith. We're made to understand that Sarah's success was because she had confidence in God's promise; knowing that God will always keep His words. In our lives as women, and as Christians, we often take our minds away from what God has revealed. We're concerned about what we see, and what we hear. Of course, these things are important, and they've been placed by God to serve their own purposes. But when it comes to trusting God, we must understand that the things we hear and see may not hold. Little wonder the Bible cautions that we live by faith and not by sight (2 Corinthians 5:7). What has God revealed about your situation? What is God's promise about your condition? What does the Lord have to say about your life's predicament? Often and on, we keep our minds locked in our intellect, in the physical and seen things. But God's revelation is all you need to thrive. It doesn't matter how long it takes, what matters is that God will surely keep His words. The Bible says that heaven and earth will fade, but His words will still remain (Matthew 24:35). A confirmation is easily noticed in Sarah's story, and in Hebrews 11:13, it is written that *these all died in faith, not having received the promises, but having seen them afar off were assured of them*. It is faith that enables you to know that God can fulfill His words even after you've died. God had promised Sarah that nations shall come from her, she only witnessed the birth of a son, but this son begot nations eventually, bringing God's promise to fulfillment.

The moment you discover God's revelation, key into it, believe it without doubt, God can bring those things to manifestation.

Now, Hebrews 11:1, we find a more widely accepted definition of faith, and as it is written, *Now faith is the substance of things hoped for, the evidence of things not seen*. Among believers, this is the definition we're all used to, and it yet illustrates the truth that faith transcends human intelligence and calculations.

More or less like saying, Yes, I do not see it, I may not feel it, but I know it will happen. This was the substance of Thomas Aquinas' claim when he said, *To one who has faith, no explanation is necessary. To one who without faith, no explanation is possible.*

Another Biblical figure also serves the purpose of explaining this definition of faith to the very details. The Bible, though unclear about God's revelation to Anna, says she was widowed barely seven years after marriage. Anna offered herself wholly to the service of God in the temple – she was a prophetess, spending the remaining days of her life in God's presence. When Jesus was presented in the temple, she was privileged to witness the birth of the long-promised messiah. She was excited because God had made this promise to her. She didn't know how and when the messiah will come, but she knew that God will make her recognize the messiah when He comes, so she remained in the temple, praying and fasting, awaiting the fulfillment of God's promise. This is found in the gospel according to Luke, Chapter 2, and verses 36 to 38:

> *Now there was one, Anna, a prophetess, the daughter of Phanuel, of the tribe of Asher. She was of great age, and had lived with a husband seven years from her virginity; and this woman was a widow of about eighty-four years, who did not depart from the temple, but served God with*

fastings and prayers night and day. And coming in that instant she gave thanks to the Lord, and spoke of Him to all those who looked for redemption in Jerusalem.

Speaking to the people about Jesus means she must have heard from God about the child, she must have received a message that kept her in the temple, waiting for its fulfillment. Such unwavering attitude towards God's promise is the pure definition of faith. You live in a daily affirmation that God is faithful, and He will definitely fulfill His words in His own time. To that end, Catherine Pulsifer says that *faith is unseen but felt, faith is strength when we feel we have none, faith is hope when all seems lost.*

Moving God to Act

Have you ever wondered what people did differently, and how they were able to get God on His feet and to act? Well, we just discussed the intricacies of faith in the last session, but faith alone doesn't save. It isn't enough to have faith that God will change situations, or that He will command forces to work in our favor; it is still pertinent to note that we have work to do. The story of Anna, as described above, shows us how it should be done. She, albeit, had faith in God, and she knew that God will surely do what He says, but she never ceased to pray.

In the words of Joni Erickson Tada, *faith isn't [just] the ability to believe long and far into the misty future. It's simply taking God at His word and taking the next step.* We're then faced with a critical question: what is this next step? It is prayer. Prayer is the means through which we bring spiritual promises into physical manifestation. It goes hand in hand with faith because you cannot pray if you do not believe God without doubt, and if you pray without faith, such a prayer is as good as pouring water on the stone. Do you remember the woman with the issue of blood in Matthew 9:20-22? The Scriptures say she made up her mind and believed that if she could touch the hem of Christ's garment, she would be healed. She didn't stop at believing this, she pushed through the overwhelming crowd that was always following Jesus; she managed to get to the point where Jesus was, and performed her planned action: touching the hem of His garment.

How many times have you believed God to convert your husband without praying about it? How often do we believe that God will soften and redirect the heart of our children, friends, and colleagues, but we never kneel to say it in prayers? How can it be that we're always quick to say that we believe that God will transform our lives, but we refuse to persevere in prayers?

We must come to God in prayers if we must receive what we seek. Definitely, God knows our every need, yet He wants us to say it with our mouth, in prayers. And like He promised in Numbers 14:28, *just as you have spoken in My hearing, so I will do to you.*

Prayer is a system through which we confess our ordinariness to God, we let God know we're weak, frail, and unable to help ourselves. It is a show of humility and total submission to God. We indirectly say to God: "I cannot handle this, but I know you're far greater than I am, and I've come to you." Prayer complements faith, and faith makes a prayer to be answered quickly.

The difference between a faithless prayer and a prayer of faith is that you already know God's revelation over your present situation, so you go ahead and remind Him of His word, and as a God who values the words of His mouth, He'll not hesitate to respond. On the other hand, if you do not have faith – you do not know God's revelation, and you do not believe it without doubt, your prayer will be hollow; it'll lack substance and is not likely to receive a response from heaven. This was the inspiration behind Charles Spurgeon's words when he said, *If you believe in prayer at all, expect God to hear you. If you do not expect, you will not have. God will not hear you unless you believe He will hear you; but if you believe He will, He will be as good as your faith.*

Prayer, as it were, is a means of communication with God. Each time we pray, we establish a connection between the heavens and the earth. Prayer draws us close to God and brings God closer than usual. When we pray, especially as women, we exchange our weakness with the strength of God, we replace depression with joy, and we take charge over unfavorable conditions. We shall see samples of this in the later chapters of this book; we shall see how prayers turn situations and how we can establish the kingdom of God on this very earth through prayer.

Our prayers, as women, are very important because just as we can bring new life into being (through childbirth), we can as well bring new things into existence. We can pray to make barren soil fertile, and we can soften the hardest of hearts through our prayers. And that takes us to another important dimension of prayer; we've all been praying, some us scream it, shout to the top of our voices, jump around in prayers, but have nothing to show for it. Perhaps, there is a specific kind of prayer that works, a kind of prayer that receives an answer. We need to learn that kind of prayer – a prayer that shakes heaven.

The Prayer that Works

In her matchless wisdom, Mother Teresa said that *God shapes the world by prayer. The more praying there is in the world, the better the world will be, the mightier the forces against evil.* However, how do we pray and get things done?

When I began to ruminate on this idea of praying the

right way, it was a bit drowning because I've always known that God searches the depth of our hearts, He knows my cares and worries. So, if I can manage to believe He can do it, and ask Him to do it, He'll surely do it. The spirit of the Lord had ministered to me, and I learned there's more to prayer. Here's what I learned:

Jesus wanted to show His disciples how to pray, and He provided what is more like a format. A shallow recitation of the Lord's Prayer doesn't show all of these, it takes a deeper explanation from the spirit of God; and even as you read it, I do hope the Lord will grant you understanding.

△ ***Our Father who is in heaven***: this is the first line in the pattern of prayer Jesus taught to His disciples, and it makes a whole lot of being beyond the words we read. The significance of this line is that we must learn to approach God as a father-figure. The Lord stands and exists as a father to all of us, He is delighted to have us come to Him, and to come as children. We are invited to go to God in prayers, not as an employee asking a manager or director for a favor, but as a little child who is approaching a loving father. In the family structure of our different societies and culture, a father is often seen as the source, provider, and sustainer; if we have this same notion about God, we can go to Him freely without considering the various factors that may say otherwise. God, in His infinite majesty, has His arms wide open anticipating the call of His daughters and/or sons. Imagine that our earthly fathers treat us with so much care and empathy, how much more, our God who is beyond all human imagination, who is neither frail nor failing. Learn today that God is a father, not a college professor that expects you to always be right. He is a loving, compassionate God, who made you; He understands you better than you understand yourself. When we have this understanding that God is our father, we can loosen up when we come before Him in prayers. We can be real with Him, speaking to Him as intimately as we would speak to our earthly fathers. *As a father pities his children, so the Lord pities those who fear Him. For He knows our frame; He remembers we're dust (Psalm 103:13-14).*

Δ ***Hallowed be Your name***: Having identified that God is our father, Jesus goes ahead to introduce a new line, and He said: *hallowed be Your name*. As I asked for the interpretation of this line, I discovered that it is an admonition not to trivialize what we have in God. Now, He is your father who always loves you; however, you must still honor Him with all your heart. While He may be gentle, loving, and understanding, never take Him for granted. It also means that we must adore God beyond the lips. Most times, when we pray, we mumble those common words that we've learned to be God's name. From a very young age, most of us memorize these things, and we do them so casually in the name of honoring God. For instance, I invited one of my students to do our opening prayer during one of our weekly fellowships, she took the microphone and immediately began to say stuff like: "You're the ancient of days, You're the mighty man in battle, You're the beginning and the end, etc." Surely, those are the qualities of God, and it is not wrong to say those sweet words to Him. Still, the question is: are they coming from your depth? Honor comes from within, it is something that is born out of outward trappings; honor comes from a place of understanding, knowing deep down you that God is really worthy of all praises. This accounts for the too many words we find in the Old and New Testament used to praise God because they all praised God according to how they encountered Him at any given time. In the case of Abraham, the Lord provided the object of sacrifice, and he [Abraham] called Him *Yireh*, which means provider. Samuel called Him *Ebenezer* because He had helped them. You see, there is an understanding, a specific revelation behind the honor accorded to God. What exactly has God done for you? What are the special ways you've encountered him? Honor Him with all your heart, with all your soul, and your prayer is bound to receive a quick answer.

Δ ***Your kingdom come, Your will be done on earth as in heaven:*** In this phase, Jesus was reminding us of the very message of salvation which is the descent of God's kingdom on this earth. When you pray, pay attention to this truth: God wants men to do His will, and doing His will means bringing His kingdom to earth. Make prayers that are in line with this agenda. Your prayers should not always be about you. Hannah, as we will soon discover in a later chapter, utilized this principle, and she got a son after many years of barrenness.

Δ ***Give us this day, our daily bread:*** God is interested in your daily affairs. You must have heard that He cares about you more than the birds of the air, and the flowers in the garden. Your responsibility is to pray to God constantly, and He'll surely be there to assist. Many of us have a once-and-for-all posture to prayer, but that isn't the way it should be. Prayer should be made daily and at any opportunity. In this regards, Joyce Meyer says, *prayer is simply talking to God like a friend and should be the easiest thing we do each day*. Keep your prayers current, and let them address present needs. This is what I mean: instead of piling up prayer points and problems, and hoping to pray about them one day, why not pray about any issue as it crops up. As soon as you encounter anything, pray about it and do not wait for a later time. In his opinion, Thomas Kinkade said, *rather than set aside daily [weekly] time for prayer, I pray constantly and spontaneously about everything I encounter on a daily basis. When someone shares something with me, I'll often simply say, "let's pray about this right now."*

Δ ***Forgive our trespasses as we forgive those who trespassed against us:*** Once more, God acknowledges that He created frail beings who will always do one or the other the wrong way. Then, He is inviting you to have the same understanding. You're dealing with mortal men, do not be surprised when they do things the wrong way because you too can do wrong to man and even to God. The message Jesus intended to pass here is that you must have a forgiving heart. No man is perfect, as they err, you forgive them and move on with your life; in this way, you're copying the character of God the most high, it becomes much easier to connect with His spirit because you're seemingly operating at the same frequency with God. This is averment to the previous invitation to seek God's will. When you easily overlook the faults of men, God will overlook your faults, and you've successfully done His will, thereby advancing His kingdom.

In essence, these are the essential things you need before going to God in prayers. They make prayers more acceptable, and they draw a speedy response from God. First is that you must acknowledge that God is your father, and you must approach Him as one. Do not go to God as one who is missing her way. Rather, be deliberate about it and know within yourself that God's fatherhood is the benefit you can always enjoy. 2 Samuel 7:14 says, *I will be his Father, and he shall be my son[daughter]*. Again, knowing that God is your father isn't an opportunity to despise Him, you must still honor Him deeply and consciously; He says in 1 Samuel 2:30 *...those who honor Me I will honor, and those who despise Me shall be lightly esteemed.* Then you must pray in line with God's will, doing His will and advancing His kingdom. Pray always and about everything, forgive people when they wrong you, *for if you forgive men their trespasses, your heavenly Father will also forgive you (Matthew 6:14)*, and you'll be ready to receive an answer from God.

In this chapter, the Lord has been able to show us how faith works and why we should always believe God without doubt. Then He also shows us that isn't enough to know that God can help, we must go to God in prayer, reminding Him of

His word, and making our requests known to Him. Finally, we've learned to make effective prayers to God for a quick response. Not all prayer works, we must pray along the pattern that Jesus taught.

Prayer

Eternal God, whose mercies are renewed every morning. I repent from all the times I refused to believe You without doubt. I am sorry for doubting You, and for questioning Your faithfulness. Help me, dear Lord, to remain steadfast in You, to love and exercise faith in Your word. Assist me as I pray from today henceforth, to pray as Jesus has taught us pray. I refuse to do things my own way, and I pledge to have my focus on doing Your will. Amen.

A Glance through Your Bible

Matthew 6:9-13; Deuteronomy 1:31-32

Matthew 6:9In this manner, therefore, pray: Our Father in heaven, Hallowed be your name. 10Your kingdom come. Your will be done on earth as it is in heaven. 11Give us this day our daily bread. 12And forgive us our debts, as we forgive our debtors. 13And do not lead us into temptation, but deliver us from the evil one. For yours is the kingdom and the power and the glory forever. Amen.

Deut. 1:31And in the wilderness where you saw how the Lord your God carried you, as a man carries his son, in all the way that you went until you came to this place. 32Yet, for all that, you did not believe the Lord your God.

Study Questions

- What does it mean to believe God **without** doubt?

- How does faith work hand-in-hand with prayer?
- What kind of prayer is answered?
- How do you move God to act?
- Why do you need to pray at all times?
- Explain the *Fatherhood* of God.

3

How to Escape the Hurdles

In our journey as Christian women, it is not new to us that prayers and faith are two important concepts. We learn from the very time we were young, that prayer is the master key. However, I have discovered that it isn't enough to know 'how-to.' How-tos are great, but there are a number of hurdles that usually stand in our way. This is often found in every sphere of human endeavor. For instance, most people know how to eat healthy, how to keep fit, how to listen to children closely, and yet, we are faced with a high number of obese people, unfit people and poor listeners. In the same way, we have great women who truly understand the Bible, they know the Scriptures inside and out, but they are not yet to apply this knowledge.

What is it that prevents people from using what they have, or applying what they know? I like to call them existential hurdles; they get in our way of developing great prayer lives, or having complete faith in Christ. A hurdle is an obstacle you're expected to overcome before you can move further from where you are. It means that if you're unable to leap over any hurdle, you get stuck at that point; and that's exactly what hurdles do to us as Christian women.

In this chapter, we're going to discuss those factors that pose hindrances to us as Christian women. When we truly understand these factors, we can take the necessary actions to keep our heads afloat.

A Leap from Your Past

The Bible gives a clear example of what it means to concentrate on your past. In Genesis Chapter 19, we find the story of Lot and his wife. The angel of the Lord had instructed them to run towards a particular direction without looking back. Of course, they obeyed the instruction up until Lot's wife looked back. The Bible records that, upon looking back, she was transformed into a pillar of salt: *But his wife looked back behind him, and she became a pillar of salt (Genesis 19:26).*

That is how many of us have turned into pillars of salts in our own lives, instead of looking forward and concentrating on what God intends to do with our lives and destiny, we let the enemy keep us grounded in the past. While it is healthy to have a rethink of where we are coming from, it is completely unhealthy to dwell on it.

God expects us to see the past, look over it, and proceed with our journey to the place of destiny. When we refuse to let go of our past – past mistakes, wrong past impressions, or any other thing in our past, we get stuck in the place of prayer.

The Bible describes the devil as the accuser of the brethren. He reminds us of the wrongs we did, and how it can hinder our prayer, but we've learned that God is a loving father whose arms are ever stretched to welcome us, He is delighted to have us come back to Him at any time. That said, your past should never be a stumbling block to your prayer life. Your past has no say when it comes to praying to God and receiving answers.

To move past these accusations that the devil hurls against us, we must take certain decisive steps to enable us to overcome our past and hold unto the glory that comes with the future.

Learn the Lesson and Move Forward!

One of my students once mustered the courage to tell me how she survived the stigma of unwanted pregnancy, she knows deep within her that it was majorly her fault, and she does not blame anyone for her misfortune. However, she recounts that it affected her prayer life when she eventually became born again. In her words, "The moment I go down on my knees in prayers, I am quickly reminded that I am a sinner, of how I wasted my younger years. I instantly feel unworthy of God's love, of God's goodness." I know this is the situation of many Christian women. We allow the devil to play with our minds and intellect. As I searched through the Scriptures, I came across an inspiring quotation from the book of Isaiah. It says, *I, even I, am He who blots out your transgressions for my own sake; and I will not remember your sins (Isaiah 43:25).*

It goes ahead to attribute God as one who makes all things new (Isaiah 65:17; Revelations 21:5). Ecclesiastes 3:11 also recorded that *He makes all things beautiful in His own time.* I like to see it as a special ability reserved for God, He understands how to replenish our faded pasts and our future which may appear bleak. Your duty as a woman is to look out for the lessons of your past. If you were, for instance, into substance abuse, you must have learned that it has health implications and that it keeps you from relating closely with your maker; now you've been delivered from this vice, you've become born again, forget them because they'll no longer make sense in your walk with God. He says in Hebrews 8:12, *For I will be merciful to their unrighteousness, and their sins and their lawless deeds I will remember no more.*

In essence, God is not interested in what happened. He is interested in what will happen. Will you learn your lessons and move forward, or will you allow the devil to cajole you into backsliding?

Quit the Blame Game

Sometimes, I really wonder what would have happened if Adam simply admitted that he had done wrong, and perhaps, asked God for mercy. The moment they had the voice of God, the Bible records they went into hiding, having known they were naked and covering themselves with leaves. Upon asking the man, he immediately pushed the blame to Eve, and when God asked Eve, she cast aspersions on the serpent.

No one wanted to be seen as the culprit. Indeed, they were both deceived into their various actions, but the most important thing is that the deed had been done. It is not time to blame anybody or exonerate yourself.

In your life's situation, I know there are people who may have harmed you, or done one thing or the other against your favor. Kindly move on, and know that blaming them will not solve your problem. At this stage, it tallies with the initial point because if you do not let go of those people, the devil keeps reminding you, yes, it was Mrs. Kate who fostered your retrenchment, it was Pete who caused you to go through the abortion process, it was your mother who didn't tell you the truth, and myriad suggestions that easily assail our minds. The Lord is saying, there is no need to blame all these people, simply accept that it happened, let go of whoever caused you pain, and let God deal with you as He wishes.

Focus on the Present

The moment God draws us from our past, He begins a massive transformation, and we become new in Him, that's why we're 'born again.' We've been put through a whole lot, and finally brought out as clean linen placed for the greater use of God. The enemy knows this, and he will always try to interfere. He brings up a lot of irrelevancies trying to steal our attention from what God is doing at the moment. You must never allow him to have his way. Put your focus on what is happening now, God is doing many things behind the scene, He reveals some to you, and keeps others away. Simply have it at the back of your mind that God is working.

Have you noticed the new kind of joy that flows in your heart? Did you not notice that you're no longer as tempered as you used to be? Has God sent help to you through your fellow women or even men? Focus on what He's doing, and you'll have no need to dwell in the past; your past, in turn, will not prevent you from making effective prayers.

Remember this: *Jesus said to him, "No one, having put his hand to the plow, and looking back, is fit for the kingdom of God"(Luke 9:62)*.

Dismantling Shame and Reproach

Shame is yet another factor that militates against our faith and prayer, especially to women. Generally, we find it difficult to be real, to be who we are; we are afraid of what people will say. So, we adopt this strategy of always changing our behaviors to *fit in*. In an attempt to fit in, we lose real touch of faith, and of our prayer life.

Shame is defined in the Oxford Dictionary as *a painful feeling of humiliation or distress caused by the consciousness of wrong or foolish behavior*. We begin to feel shame when we do something that isn't right in the sight of God, and of man. But the truth is, shame is not an idea we should ever allow a foothold in our lives. A preacher once used a story of a little boy in his sermon, and I've reproduced it here with little emphasis so we can fully dissect the idea of shame and its implications. Let me call this boy Tom.

Tom was the last child of his parents, he had most of his laundry done by older siblings and his mom. When he became old enough to handle his clothes, mom told him to take out his dirty clothes and get them washed, washing machines weren't commonplace like today, so everyone had to wash manually. Tom wasn't keen, and he always had a difficult time washing his own clothes. He came up with a strategy that worked a while before boomeranging; Tom hid some of his dirty clothes under the mattress, he will do this, hoping to have only a few clothes to wash, and to keep the dirty ones away from mom's sight. He felt smart, and his idea worked! But, it didn't take long before piece of clothes began to accumulate under the mattress – the mattress became uneven and went hanging. You can guess what happened next: he couldn't hide any more clothes, and mom discovered what he'd been doing, she mandated him to bring them and wash once. What can we deduce from this? He did wrong by hiding those clothes, he was ashamed of letting mom know he hid the clothes, and he continues to hide them just to avoid notice!

This story illustrates what happens to us when we're ashamed, we begin to look for ways to cover up. When Adam and Eve erred, they hid themselves, covering up themselves with fig leaves. The Lord is saying, there is no need to cover up things, as you continue to cover, you'll keep on sinking into the pit of low self-esteem and a complete disconnection from God. No matter how much you try, whatever covering you place over wrongdoings will tear part one day, and the effect may be disastrous.

Again, shame will only draw you farther from God. This happens when you take steps that are completely antithetical to the ways of God, out of shame for your action or inaction. You know you did wrong, but instead of running to God for help, you seek help where there is none.

If you want to deal with shame, then realize that God is already aware: isn't it ridiculous that we want to hide from the maker of the universe? The Bible says in Hebrews 4:13, *there is no creature hidden from His sight, but all things are naked and open to the eyes of Him to whom we must give account.* He knows all you've done, covering up does no good. Once you realize that God knows all about you, then you will be real with Him without feeling shame.

He isn't a man that can take your story and announce abroad. He is not a preacher who may use your story for a sermon. He is the Lord of heavens, the holy one of Israel who will always remember you're dust. God's love overlooks your sins: having known that God is aware of your faults, you must also realize that His love supersedes your sins, He loves you for simply being his creation, not because of good deeds. Remember He loved us even while we were yet sinners (Romans 5:8). In his song titled *This God Is Too Good*, an African songwriter and singer, Nathaniel Bassey, captures the love of God thus:

I know a God, who's merciful and kind

> *Faithful and gracious*
> *I'm the apple of His eyes*
> *The thought that fills His heart*
> *Every morning, noon and night*
> *He loved me when I didn't care*
> *And was patient till I came*
> *Running back into His arms*
> *Look how He turned my life around*
> *Made me a shining star*
> *His glory to reveal*

Notice that God loved you, even when you didn't care. I trust God will help you embrace this truth, and always run to Him in all openness. Never try to hide from God!

Do Not Be Ridiculed into Silence

Lectures had ended for the day; students were headed for various destinations, some to their dorms, some to the library, some just hanging around. On Tuesdays, my few Christian friends and I usually gather around a particular hall for a short meeting before we get dispatched for an hour-long evangelism. Though we were students, we did understand that preaching the good news was the duty of all Christians. We set out a few hours on Tuesday evenings (after a brief meeting), and we go around speaking to random people about Christ. On this Tuesday, we had a 'new convert' in our midst, she recently gave her life to Christ, and she had enormous zeal to spread the message. The leader tried to dissuade her, telling her that she needed a little more time to know more, dig deeper into the Scriptures before embarking on any kind of evangelism. She was persistent, and when the leader noticed she could never be convinced, she allowed her.

When we gathered again to share our experience, this 'new convert' stepped forth and told us how she met old friends and people with whom she had wandered in the wilderness; upon seeing her with a Bible, and noticing that she now preaches, they laughed out loud, mocking the genuineness of her over-night repentance. She narrated that one of her old friends said to her, "you're a pot, you cannot call a kettle black." Many of us, especially myself, thought she would break down, and that she might quit fellowshipping with us, but instead she said, "It is not worth the peace and love of Christ that I've found. I didn't reply them, and I will not let myself be ridiculed into silence."

Wow! I got utterly astounded. She would not let herself be ridiculed into silence. I immediately thought of the many times I refused to do certain things because I felt I might be ridiculed by people who know me, or know my dark past.

I learned that we must look beyond the ridicules of men. Maybe, you use to be a troublemaker teen, or a bad mother; then you eventually found Christ who altered everything and gave you a new life, but your loved ones don't accept it yet, they think you're still the untrustworthy kind of lady. Each time you pray in the house, or fast from food, or prepare for fellowship, they smirk at you, and say, "Pretenders in the house of God," you must understand that it is in the nature of human beings to judge. They want to make you feel guilty so that they can control you and your emotions. Do not allow that to happen, with time, they'll find no more reason to despise you.

While on the cross, one of the robbers who was crucified with Jesus said to Him, *If you are the Christ, save Yourself and save us (Luke 23:39)*. But it didn't stop Jesus from completing His mission, in fact, He granted pardon and paradise to the second criminal who asked for it. In the same way, you will be derided for your prayerfulness, for your faith in God, do not be dismayed.

I often give a response to my friends when they ask for certain things, and that is: Let me pray about it. To them, it is too much, and I am supposed to make an instant decision. They will always say one thing or the other to make me skip the 'pray-about-it,' but it'll never happen. I know why I pray, and I know who I pray to, the ridicule of other people will not make me go silent.

Courage: A Message from Ruth

Ruth can be a great inspiration to women of all times, not because she had enormous physical strength, or outstandingly beautiful, but because she possessed an uncommon kind of courage. The Bible records that she was married to one out of the two sons of Naomi. These men (sons of Naomi) died; their father, Elimelech had also died, leaving Naomi with her two daughters-in-law. Naomi adjudged herself cursed, and declared that the hand of the Lord has gone against her (Ruth 1:13). Finally, she set to return to Bethlehem in Judah, from where they had fled for fear of famine.

The striking thing is that Ruth opted to follow Naomi back to Judah. As a matter of fact, she was a young widow without a child, she had the opportunity of going back to her father's house and perhaps, getting married to another man – she was a beautiful woman. But Ruth decided otherwise, she said, *Entreat me not to leave you, or turn back from following after you; for wherever you go, I will go; and wherever you lodge, I will lodge; your people shall be my people, and your God, my God (Ruth 1:16).*

What Ruth meant by those words were beyond leaving her land (Moab) to a new place, it means she is going to become a stranger, she will forfeit her culture, her faith as a Moabite, and she is going to a place where her future is not secured. This kind of courage is not just unusual, it is inspiring. We must understand that she had no background in the Jewish system of worshipping God, she didn't know God, yet, she was willing to take on this sojourn to an unknown destination. Ruth's experience shows a number of truths, she found God through her mother-in-law, and she wasn't really ready to let go. She followed her instructions very closely, and she eventually had her reward beyond expectations.

In your life, as a Christian woman, do you have enough courage to face troubles as they come? They will surely come in various guises, and if you do not have the courage to withstand these things, you end up falling out of track.

For instance, you've just been dismissed from your job, you have no other source of income, you have a sick child, and you haven't paid your rent. The natural response is always grief, we become unable to grapple with the situation. It is situations like this that make many women (and men) turn atheists. At a point, they feel that God has deserted them and that the entire God-thing is no longer working. It should never be same with you, you must be willing and courageous enough to face challenges as they come, and you must know that God does not plot mischief.

Like Ruth, you must be willing to leave those things behind and go to God in prayer. It doesn't matter how overwhelming your predicament may be, you must still go to God in prayers. Never allow the troubles of this world to make you leave the path of righteousness, ignore your prayer life, or lose faith in God.

Prayer

Holy God, eternal owner of all that exists, I thank You for opening my eyes to these things. I've learned them, and I declare that my ugly past, my shame or reproach, my troubles and circumstances will never cause me to stop praying. Help me, by the power of Your grace, to stand firm, and to always run towards You, not away from You. Amen

A Glance through Your Bible

Isaiah 43: 18-19; Proverbs 4:25; 2 Timothy 2:26

Isaiah 43:18Do not remember the former things, nor consider the things of old. ¹⁹Behold, I will do a new thing, now it shall spring forth; shall you not know it? I will even make a road in the wilderness and rivers in the desert.

Proverbs 4:25Let your eyes look straight ahead, and your eyelids look right before you.

2 Timothy 2:26 And that they may come to their senses and escape the snare of the devil, having been taken captivity by him to do his will.

Study Questions

- Does your past define you in Christ?
- What should you do when you feel shame?
- Why is it dangerous to look back?

4

Aligning to the Will of God

The question of the will of God is one, I have observed, and baffles many Christians, irrespective of gender or denomination. I once met Susan at a conference where I was invited to speak to a group of Christian married women. The conference was divided into two sessions: the first allowed speakers to speak the whole time, while the second was more of an interactive session. At the interactive session, the participants were given the floor to ask questions on issues relating to them as Christian married women.

For about the first 50 minutes of the scheduled 2-hour session, questions bordering on different areas relating to women were asked. Susan, a married woman, probably in her mid-30s, raised her hand, wearing a rather puzzled look on her face, and asked: "how exactly can we know the will of God concerning our prayers and the decisions we make?" This question was like a paradigm shift to the pattern of questions asked so far. For the remainder of the session, every question asked were directly or indirectly related to the same thing

Susan had asked. This was a clear sign that the few minutes answer we gave was anything but sufficient enough to satisfy their deep-seated confusion on the subject.

The knowledge of God's will is definitely an essential part of Christianity and Christian living. How else are we supposed to know what steps to take at certain crossroads of our lives or whether or not to believe God for something we desire? Hence, the lack of a clear and precise understanding of what God wills for us is not only a potential stumbling block to our Christian living, it is also a threat to our faith.

At the end of the conference session, Susan walked up to me, seeking clarification on what God's will means. She admitted her question hadn't been exactly answered. I spent a few minutes trying to help her understand. Eventually, we exchanged contacts, and I had to try to answer her question over the next few days, supplying her with relevant study materials to help in her quest. Not too long later, when we spoke on the phone, she sounded a lot more confident than the Susan I met at the conference. This time, she told me on the phone: "I am now constantly learning to align my desires to the will of God." How else could she have thought about aligning to the will of God if she has not had clear and precise knowledge about it in the first place?

The apostle John speaks about the huge role the knowledge of the will of God plays in the effectiveness of our prayer life. He says: *Now this is the confidence that we have in Him, that if we ask anything according to His will, He hears us (1 John 5:14).* How else could we pray according to His will without understanding what really He wills for us? Jesus constantly spoke about doing the will of the Father who had sent Him: ... *I do not seek My own will, but the will of the Father who sent Me (John 5:30).* Similarly, we are not expected to pray according to our own will or desires without considering its alignment to the will of God.

What Is the Will of God?

The subject of the will of God constantly features in the writings of the apostle Paul. One of his most outstanding references is found in his epistle to the Romans: *do not be conformed to this world, but be ye transformed by the renewing of your mind, that you may prove what is that good and acceptable and perfect will of God* (Romans 12:2).

By this expression, "do not be conformed to the world," Paul seems to say that the will of God may not be the conventional ideas that we may have acquired in the secular world. From his usage of the phrase in several other passages, we find him refer to specific conducts: *Do not be unwise, but understand (Ephesians 5:17).* Discerning the will of the Lord is not a matter of feeling or emotion, but of mental understanding, applying our minds to Scripture, explains *NKJV Study Bible*. The following verses prove what he means as he refers to specific conducts: *be filled with the Spirit (Ephesians 5:18), wives, submit to your husbands, as to the Lord*

(Ephesians 5:22), husbands, love your wives (Ephesians 5:25), etc. The explanation, "discerning the will of the Lord…, applying our minds to the Scripture," thus, makes it clear to us that the will of God is basically found in His Word.

In his epistle, the apostle Peter sheds some light on the will of God, further helping us understand Paul's contextual usage. Peter says: *For this is the will of God, that by doing good, you may put to silence the ignorance of foolish men (1 Peter 2:15).* When we read contextually, we'll also find out that Peter is referring to specific godly conducts. The epistle of John further sheds more light, making reference to the will of God as doing God's word. In his words, *the world is passing away, and the lust of it, but he who does the will of God abides forever (1 John 2:17).*

The will of God, as used in the New Testament, refers to God's divine purpose, desire, pleasure, etc. While it is often used in reference to our conducts, it is also used, a lot of times, to refer to what God has done. Paul, for instance, often referred to himself as called as "an apostle by the will of God" (1 Corinthians 1:1, Ephesians 1:1, and Colossians 1:1). Also, the provision of salvation for us in Christ Jesus is identified as a function of God's will (Ephesians 1:5). Another popular usage of the will of God refers to what God wants for us.

Jeremiah 29:11 gives us an idea of what God's desire for our lives is: *For I know the thoughts that I think towards you, says the Lord, thoughts of peace, and not of evil, to give you a future and a hope.* In the New Testament, we find Jesus speaking about the heavenly father's constant willingness to give good things to those who ask him (Matthew 7:11). The apostle John echoes this same desire in his letter to Gaius: *I pray that you may prosper in all things and be in health, just as your soul prospers (3 John 1:2).*

In summary, the will of God entails His desires for our conduct and our lives, as found in His word. From the life of Jesus, as our example and the teachings in the epistles, we can tell the will of God for our conducts. We can also tell, from the promises of God for us through Scriptures, what He desires for our lives. Hence, aligning ourselves to the will of God is ensuring that our prayer life and relationship with others is aligned to God's will. Surely, when we pray in line with God's will, we can be sure that He hears and answers us.

When we make requests for specific things that we desire, knowing that it is the will of God to give it to us, our faith is strengthened. A lady, who identified herself as Sara, sent me an email about her lack of certainty on whether or not her marriage was God's will. She claimed her husband had suddenly become a drunk in just less than a year into the marriage. He seemed to have suddenly lost interest in the marriage, and would often stay away from home for days. Their communication had degenerated into constant acrimonious arguments. According to the email she sent me, she had been praying about this situation for several weeks, and it only seemed to be getting worse. At this point, she was almost sure her marriage wasn't God's will.

Most of the times, our negative perception of God's will is responsible for our doubts in the place of prayer. I could tell, from Sara's email, that her prayer had been devoid of the confidence that God was interested in answering her. I replied, letting her know that marriage is God's will, and that it was established throughout Scriptures. I also let her know that it was God's will for her to have a happy and fruitful marriage. From a few exchange of email later on, I could tell that, not only was she not confident of God's will for her, she hadn't aligned herself with the will of God for her marriage. Her love for her husband had grown cold, and she had taken it upon herself to interrogate him constantly. She always started the arguments every time her husband was home.

We must understand that the will and desire of God for every facet of our life is good. However, we also have to carry out will and desires for our conducts. The apostle Peter gives a very effective marriage recipe to wives in his epistle. In his words, *wives, likewise, be submissive to your own husbands, that even if some do not obey the word, they, without a word, may be won by the conduct of their wives (1 Peter 3:1)*. I showed Sara this part of Scripture, supporting it with another very similar nugget from James: *...submit to God. Resist the devil and he'll flee from you (James 4:7)*. I let her know that by being loving and caring towards her husband, she is submitting to God. Thus, not only will she be likely to influence her husband positively, she would be able to resist the power of the enemy over her marriage through her prayers. Doing this, I told her, is aligning herself with the will of God.

After I supplied her with this recipe, Sara went ahead to put it to work. She changed her conducts towards her husband, chose to love him despite his wrongs, and continued praying. This time, she prayed more confidently that it was God's will for her to have a happy marriage. In just about three months, she sent me a mail of gratitude. She had been able to transform herself, her husband, and their marriage! They had gone to see a therapist together, and have had all their issues addressed. The lesson is that all she needed was to, first, align herself with the will of God for her conducts. Consequently, it was easier to unleash the power of her prayer. It became clear that her prayers had always been effective.

Your Prayers Are Effective

The tendency to think our prayers are not heard is one of the constant threats to our faith when we pray. Many people are unable to receive or recognize the answers to their prayers due to this pattern of thinking. James gives us a clue into the potential harms of not recognizing the effectiveness of our prayers. He says: *…let him ask of God who gives to all liberally and without reproach, and it will be given to him. But let him ask in faith, with no doubting, for he who doubts is like a wave of the sea driven and tossed by the wind (James 1: 5-6).*

One key effect of doubt is the fact that it makes it difficult to recognize and work with the answers that God has given us.

Just as James says, doubts will make us double-minded, tossed to and fro. If you allow it, doubts make it impossible for your mind to be settled in the promises of God, thus, making you uninspired to take appropriate steps. However, confidence in the effectiveness of your prayers will definitely help you get your desired results fast enough. If Sara had continued doubting that her prayers were not effective and that God wasn't interested in answering them, she would surely not have taken the necessary steps she took, as effectively as she did. Confidence in the fact that your prayers are effective may just be all you need to get all the answers that you desire.

In the words of Clement Stone, *prayer is man's greatest power*. This means it is beyond just a religious activity that we do to make ourselves feel good about ourselves or whatsoever situation we are going through. Our prayers are effective weapons by which we can be able to make changes in our world. E. M. Bounds bears witness to this fact in his words: *Prayer is the greatest of all forces, because it honors God and brings Him into active aid.* The point is that God always hears us every time we ask. Just as John says *...if we ask anything according to His will, He hears us (1 John 5:14).* As long as we are aligned to his will, our prayers are surely effective.

One of the most popular parts of Scripture on the effectiveness of prayer is found in the epistle of James. *The effectual fervent prayer of a righteous man avails much (James 5:16b).* This simply means that your prayers are effective.

James makes this clearer in the following verses: *Elijah was a man with a nature like ours, and he prayed earnestly that it would not rain; and it did not rain on the land for three years and six months. And he prayed again, and the heaven gave rain, and the earth produced its fruit (James 5:17-18).* As people of the same nature, we can pray and have our prayers completely answered. If Elijah was able to influence nature by virtue of his prayers, why would it be impossible to cause changes in our own individual lives?

The Bible is replete with the stories of women who stood their ground in faith, prayed and had got the results of their prayers. Names like Deborah, Hannah, Esther, Anna, etc. easily come to mind. However, in reading the stories of these women, we can see that they believed in the efficiency of their prayers. They believed that God was concerned about their welfare. Their trust in God's faithfulness to supply their wants when they pray is definitely the key factor to the answered prayers. Hence, trusting in the efficiency of our prayers is definitely fundamental.

Staying in Faith

A lot of negative experiences or fear that we have acquired over time may pose an impediment to our confidence in God's word. You have probably heard from or about other people who were in your situation, and didn't have their prayers answered. Well, it depends on what you choose to see. Faith demands that we look only at the positives and stick to it. The Bible speaks about Abraham, the father of faith, as our example. And not being weak in faith, he did not consider his own body already dead (since he was about a hundred years old) and the deadness of Sarah's womb. He did not waver at the promises of God through unbelief, but was strengthened in faith, giving glory to God-(Romans 4: 19-20). You may just need to consider the same thing.

Now, staying in faith goes beyond clenching your fist, trying to muster-up some confidence, etc. It is beyond your physical or emotional wherewithal. Faith primarily stems from resting on the promises of God's word. In fact, God's word is the origin of faith. *So then, faith comes by hearing, and hearing by the word of God (Romans 10:17).* Now, you'll agree with me that if faith comes by hearing, it is very likely that fear also comes by hearing. In other words, if faith comes by hearing God's word, fear is very likely to come from hearing that which is the opposite of God's word. Anything that contradicts God's will, desires, and promises for us is very much likely to create fear within us.

The right step to take towards maintaining faith is to cultivate the culture of minding what comes into our minds and hearts. The book of Proverbs succinctly summarizes this to us in the words: *Keep your heart with all diligence, for out of it spring the issues of life (Proverbs 4:23).* Now, keeping our hearts can be done by consciously watching the information we allow into it. Hanging out with people who do nothing but bring down our confidence in God's promises and desires for us is definitely not safe. Hence, ensuring that you surround yourself with people, reading materials, television shows, etc. that uplift your faith is just the right approach to ensuring that you constantly stay in faith. The apostle Paul admonishes us on this:

> *Finally, brethren, whatever things are true, whatever things are noble, whatever things are just, whatever things are pure, whatever things are lovely, whatever things are of good report, if there be any virtue and if there is anything praiseworthy – meditate on these things (Philippians 4: 8).*

It is not God's responsibility to help us stay in faith. It is our responsibility to build the perfect environment to help our faith thrive, by fellowshipping with the right persons and materials. Also, by consciously choosing the thoughts that we welcome, it is easier for us to be settled on the promises of God's word and to stay in faith.

What If He Doesn't Answer

The question of whether or not our prayers will be answered is one that constantly comes to us intermittently. Sometimes, it is a product of our rational minds seeking to find an indubitable reason to believe that our prayers would be answered. At other times, we are subconsciously looking out for an alternative to stick to if it turns out that God doesn't answer our prayers. Even though this thought is normal and virtually every praying Christian can relate to it, it is important to not accommodate it for too long. This is because it may hurt our faith. Thus, a perfect response to this question, when it comes into our minds, is "what if He answers?"

The nature of God isn't consistent with not answering our prayers. Jesus revealed a Father who is ever ready to listen to our prayers and to answer them. ...Most assuredly, *I say unto you, whatever you ask the Father in My name, He will give you... Ask, and you will receive, that your joy may be full (John 16: 23-24)*. He is ever willing and ready to give what we ask to us. This brings to mind what the apostle John says: ...*if we ask anything according to His will, He hears us (1 John 5:14)*. John concludes this in the following verse thus: *And if we know that He hears us, whatever we ask, we know that we have the petitions that we desired of Him (1 John 5:15)*. How remarkable! John speaks about knowing that we have the petitions that we desired of him. Now, that is resting on His promises.

With the knowledge that God is ever ready to answer our prayers, we can always stay in faith. Now, it is truly not uncommon to be faced with situations that make it seem as though our prayers are not being answered. This is particularly rampant at times when you are making time-bound requests. You often tend to think, "well, God, you've got to hurry up now." A lot of times, we feel disappointed when we do not get our requests at the time we hope to get them. Your dashed hope for a specific "blessing" before the end of the year is likely to make you think: "well, God did not answer." Experiences like this make you ask yourself, at other times, "what if He doesn't answer?"

The story of Lazarus is one of the most inspiring of the gospel of John. Lazarus was sick, and his sisters had no choice but to send for Jesus to come heal him. Jesus promptly responded, *this sickness is not unto death but for the glory of God (John 11:4).* Well, as it turned out, Lazarus died. His sisters, having received the message of Jesus to them, must have thought: "well, Jesus' prayer didn't work this time." Eventually, Jesus went to Judea, where Lazarus had now been buried for four days. Upon seeing Him, Martha, one of Lazarus' sisters, met Him, telling Him, *Lord, if you had been here, my brother would not have died (John 11:21).* Martha must have concluded that there was no longer a way out. Her brother was now dead and buried for four days! Even when Jesus assured her that her brother, Lazarus, would rise again, her response only showed she had concluded there was no longer a way out. *I know that he will rise again in the resurrection at the last day (John 11:24).*

Mary and Martha must have concluded that God had not answered their prayer for their sick brother to be healed.

Well, to any rational being, it would appear "God did not answer." However, one inspiring thing about Martha is her resolute faith in Christ. Despite her state of disappointment at her brother's death, she still chose to express her faith in Him.

Jesus said unto her, "I am the resurrection and the life. He who believes in Me, though he may die, he shall live. And whosoever lives and believes in Me shall never die. Do you believe this?" She said to Him, **"Yes, Lord, I believe that You are the Christ, the Son of God, who is to come into the world."**

Even though Lazarus had been dead and buried for four days, and all hope was lost on him living again, Jesus raised him back to life (John 11: 43-44). This was what we would call, in today's terms, "worst-case scenario." Still, God was still had a way out. Every time I meditate on this story, I get inspired to keep my faith and trust in Him. In the face of a situation where an urgent miracle is required, I always choose to remain unfazed. I am constantly sure that God cannot be limited by time. Even in the face of approaching deadlines, I silence the doubts in my mind by reminding myself that God is bigger than the deadline.

When you are faced with thoughts of "what if He doesn't answer," all you have to do is to remind yourself of the fact that God loves you. Choose to meditate on Jesus' description of Him as a father who will give you what you ask of Him. Also, remind yourself that He is not bound by any limitation whatsoever. He is greater than time, matter and space, and would go beyond all these to meet you at the point of your needs.

The Hannah Secret

Your stance during difficult and tempting situations are very fundamental to your eventual results. Choosing to be calm and unruffled at times when we have every reason to vent out our frustration is an invaluable faith posture. The story of Hannah is a very clear proof of this. Hannah is not only one of the most inspiring women in the Bible, but she is also one of the most astounding personalities. Her faith, conduct, prayerfulness, etc. are examples that have been relevant throughout history. Hannah's story is one from which we can learn tons of lessons which have the capacity to transform both our prayer lives and our conduct during trials and difficult times.

Elkanah was married to two wives, Hannah and Peninnah (Note that Polygamy was accepted and practiced by ancient Israelites). While Hannah had no child, her rival, Peninnah had children. However, despite her childlessness, Elkanah, Hannah's husband, loved her specially and often showed it. Her rival, Peninnah, thus, made her life miserable and constantly mocked her for her childlessness.

And her rival provoked her severely to make her miserable… So it was, year by year, when she went up to the house of the Lord, that she provoked her, therefore she wept and did not eat (1 Samuel 1: 6-7).

In her desperation for a child, Hannah went to the House of the Lord, Shiloh, to pray. She prayed so hard with "bitterness of soul" and "anguish" (1 Samuel 1:10). One very noticeable fact here is that there was no record of complaint or lament. Despite her frustrations, she didn't blame God for keeping her childless. Rather, she chose to make a vow. Then she made a vow and said, *"O Lord of hosts, if You will indeed look on the affliction of Your maidservant and remember me, and not forget Your maidservant, but will give Your maidservant a male child, then I will give him to the Lord all the days of his life…"* She knew there was a God to hear her vows, relate with her pains, and answer her.

Hannah's prayer was so intense that Eli, the priest, thought she was drunk. *How long will you be drunk? Put your wine away from you (1 Samuel 1: 14),* Eli said. But Hannah responded ever so calmly: *No, my lord, I am a woman of sorrowful spirit. I have drunk neither wine nor intoxicating drink, but have poured out my soul before the Lord* (1 Samuel 1:15). In her sadness and bitterness of soul, Hannah could have chosen to respond angrily to Eli's unfair accusations. It could have been a little understandable if she had decided to vent out a little of her frustrations at that point. She could, at least, have chosen to ignore him. But, she knew better. She understood that it was important to honor the priest of God. She, thus, chose to respond with so much honor. She didn't let her frustrations get the better part of her. She chose to stick with the right conducts. This paid off massively.

Then Eli answered and said, "Go in peace, and the God of Israel grant your petition which you have asked of Him. And she said, "Let your maidservant find favor in your sight." So the woman went her way and ate, and her face was no longer sad (1 Samuel 1: 17-18). This was all the encounter that Hannah needed. It didn't take too long later for her to conceive and give birth to her son, Samuel. Now, in line with her vow, she waited for Samuel to get weaned and took him to the house of the Lord, with offerings, and made him remain there. It didn't take too long for God to bless Hannah with other children. *And the Lord visited Hannah, so that she conceived and bore three sons and two daughters (1 Samuel 2:21).* Her shame and reproach were gone!

One very notable lesson in Hannah's story is her total alignment to the will of God. When she prayed intensely for a child, the will of God must have also been paramount in her mind. Instead of making a vow to give offerings and sacrifices to God, she pledged her son to the service of God instead. It is quite clear that she didn't desire a son for selfish reasons. Another astounding lesson to learn from her is her trust in God to answer prayers. When she was spited by her rival, Peninnah, she simply decided to go to God in prayers. She stayed at the house of the Lord, praying hard, until Eli, the priest, blessed her request and encouraged her to go home. She believed that God was able to respond to her prayers.

Hannah's conduct is yet another demonstration of her alignment to the will of God. There is no Scripture evidence that she was vindictive against her rival, Peninnah, for mocking her. She responded respectfully and with so much honor when Eli dismissively referred to her as a drunken woman. Also, after Samuel was born, she promptly took him to serve in the house of the Lord as she had earlier pledged. She was simply passionate about the will of God.

While we pray, we also need to be conscious of the will of God as it regards our conducts and the plans of God for our lives or the situations in which we seek to effect changes through prayers. When we are sure that our prayers are in perfect sync with the will of God, our faith is a lot more effective. Also, by ensuring that our conducts are in line with what God desires of us, we can be sure that we are on the right path to answered prayers

Prayer

Dear Father, I believe that You are faithful, and that Your promises are ever dependable. I choose to submit myself to Your will in my prayers, conducts, and thoughts. I choose to stay in faith always, trusting in Your love for me and Your power to meet my needs per time. I ask that You open the eyes of my understanding to comprehend Your will for my life at every point in time. Amen.

A Glance through Your Bible

1 John 5: 13-15; Jeremiah 29:11

John 5:13 These things I have written to you who believe in the name of the Son of God, that you may know that you have eternal life, and that you may *continue to* believe in the name of the Son of God. 14 Now this is the confidence that we have in Him, that if we ask anything according to His will, He hears us. 15 And if we know that He hears us, whatever we ask, we know that we have the petitions that we have asked of Him.

____

____

Jeremiah 29: 11 For I know the thoughts that I think toward you, says the Lord, thoughts of peace and not of evil, to give you a future and a hope.

Study Questions

- What is the importance of knowing the will of God to our prayer life?
- What does it mean to align oneself to God's will?
- What is the importance of the right conducts to one's prayer life?
- How can one stay in faith in the face of difficulties?
- Why is it important to know that our prayers are effective?

5

The Ministry of Intercession

I am not the greatest follower or fan of the game of soccer, but I do enjoy spending some of my spare time, at weekends, watching some soccer action on TV. Now, one thing that I really find enjoyable about the game is its natural emphasis on teamwork. The need to have the ball passed around the field, from one player to another, seems impossible to ignore if a team is to keep the ball. When some player tries to do the job alone, dribbling past the opposing players, he opens himself and the team to the risk of losing the ball. And from my observation, it appears that the most successful teams in the game have greater levels of cohesion and cooperation, compared to their opponents. Now, isn't this just the same case with every other kind of team?

If you have ever been a part of any successful team, one fundamental lesson you must have learned is the importance of cooperation. Cooperation is evidently the basic operating principle for any successful team. The idea of a team, in the first place, entails the cooperation of a group of people. It is about the working or striving together of a people towards the achievement of a specific common goal. Now, cooperation is not only found in sports teams or business organizations, it is a quality that it is indispensable to our relationship as Christians.

The analogy, "body of Christ," is one that is constantly used through Scripture when describing the church, or body of Christians. A classic example of this usage is found in the apostle Paul's letter to the Romans: ...*So we, being many, are one body in Christ, and individually members of one another (Romans 12:5)*. Now, the most likely reason for this expression is to communicate the spiritual synchrony and unity of the church. It is in line with this pattern of thinking that Paul establishes his teachings on the need for Christians to work together and cooperate in their responsibilities. The following verses of Romans 12:5 show this. I find verses 10, 11, and 16 quite noteworthy.

Be kindly affectionate to one another with brotherly love, in honor giving preference to one another; not lagging in diligence, fervent in spirit, serving the Lord... Be of the same mind towards one another. Do not set your mind on high things, but associate with the humble. Do not be wise in your own opinion (Romans 12: 10-11, 16).

Again, more precisely, the epistle to the Philippians reflects the need for the cooperation of Christians, particularly as it concerns the ministry of the gospel: *...stand fast in one spirit, with one mind striving together for the faith of the gospel (Philippians 1:27)*. What this shows is that the contribution of everyone is required, in one way or the other, as it regards the ministry of the gospel. Everyone surely has a part to play.

One of the key areas in which Christian cooperation is needed is in the ministry of intercession. The need to make prayers for fellow Christians, those in authority and, generally, all humans, is a very recurrent theme in the Scriptures. A classic example is found in 1 Timothy 2:1-2 which says: *Therefore, I exhort first of all that supplications, prayers, intercessions, and giving of thanks be made for all men, for kings, and all that are in authority that we may lead a quiet and peaceable life in all godliness and reverence*. Now, this request is not a strange one, considering the fact that Jesus Himself had set the pace.

Jesus Christ walked the earth, not only as our savior, but also as our example. Basically, we are His imitators (Ephesians 5: 1-2). Now, throughout the accounts of the gospel books (Matthew, Mark, Luke, and John), it is not uncommon to see verses that speak about Jesus separating Himself to the wilderness to pray. Once, He told Peter, *Simon Simon! Indeed, Satan has asked for you... But I have prayed for you, that your faith should not fail (Luke 22: 31-33)*. This only proves to us that several times he prayed, he was interceding. The apostle Paul is another example of an intercessor. In several parts of his epistles, he expressed how much he prays for other Christians. To the Ephesians, he says, *I do not cease to give thanks for you, making mention of you in my prayers (Ephesians 1:16).* He also told the Colossian church: *...We... do not cease to pray for you, and to ask that you may be filled with the knowledge of His will... (Colossians 1:9).* We, as Christians, are also entrusted with the responsibility to pray and intercede for others.

The New Testament epistles are replete with requests for the prayers of the church. On some occasions, the apostles themselves were the ones in need of the prayers of the church. The writer of Hebrews, in his letter, says, *Pray for us (Hebrews 13:18).* The epistle to the Thessalonians reads, *Pray for us (1 Thessalonians 3:1).* The epistle to the Colossians also reads: *praying also for us... (Colossians 4:3).* Several other times, we are required to pray for other believers. James writes, in his epistle: *...and pray for one another (James 5:16).* The epistle to the Ephesians also requests that Christians be *watchful... with all perseverance and supplication for all saints (Ephesians 5:18).*

When we, as believers, maintain our responsibility as intercessors, so much can be done. When we cooperatively stand our ground in the place of prayer, we are definitely empowered to get answers. Jesus lets us know this: *...if two of you shall agree on earth concerning anything they shall ask, it shall be done for them... (Matthew 18:21).*

Women and the Ministry of Intercession

Women have featured through recent and ancient history as key intercessors for the church. Also, there are records in the Scriptures, regarding how women have served as key intercessors. A very notable story is that of the prophetess, Anna. *She was of great age, and had lived with a husband seven years from her virginity, and this woman was a widow of about eighty-four years, who did not depart from the temple, but served God with fastings and prayers night and day (Luke 2: 36-37).* She had lived the greater part of her life, serving God with fastings and prayers in the temple. One thing to note is the fact that she must have spent her prayer times praying for any other thing, but herself. Anna had to have been an intercessor, to have been recognized as someone who "served God" with her fastings and prayers.

The book of Acts tells one of the most remarkable stories on the power of prayer and intercession when done cooperatively. Herod had killed James, John's brother, who, thus, became the first of Jesus' twelve apostles to die for the gospel. When James was killed, and Herod saw that the Jews were pleased with it, he proceeded to take Peter also, kept him in prison, with the intention to kill him. The Bible, however, records that *constant prayer was offered to God for him by the church (Acts 12: 5).* Eventually, the night before the day Herod intended to have him killed, Peter was miraculously delivered by the ministry of an angel. Thanks to the constant and unwavering prayer of the church for him!

Now, here is the interesting detail: when Peter was delivered, *he came to the house of Mary, the mother of John… where many were gathered together praying (Acts 12:12)*. It turns out that Mary, the mother of John, was the one who hosted the gathering of the church! Apparently, she was a key figure in the organizing of the other believers for prayers. She was a leading intercessor! When Peter knocked at the door, it was a young girl named Rhoda, who came to answer her (verse 13). Apparently, she was a part of the prayer. Bible scholars argue that, given the names listed in the passage, there are likely to have been far more women than men in the gathering for prayers. Thus, it is also arguable that this early church, in the days of the Apostles, had key intercessors who were women!

Post-biblical church history is also replete with the stories of women who have altered the course of their days and generations through unwavering prayers. They include Monica (Augustine's mother), Susanna Wesley (John and Charles Wesley's mother), Fenny Crosby (hymn writer), and several more.

Standing in the Gap

I find the term, *"stand in the gap"* (Ezekiel 22:30), a perfect expression for what it truly means to intercede. It somewhat expresses the role of an advocate or "defense attorney." It is about standing between the accusation or accuser and the one who is accused. The typical advocate will stop at nothing to ensure that the defendant is cleared of the accusations laid against him/her. Basically, he/she is passionate about getting the accused out of trouble. It is based on this understanding that the apostle John refers to Jesus Christ as our advocate with the father: *And if anyone sins, we have an Advocate with the Father, Jesus Christ the righteous (1 John 2:1).*

Now, the major responsibility of an intercessor is to stand in the gap between the trouble and the one who is about to get into it. Now, this is done in the place of constant intercession for the concerned party. It can be an individual or a group of people. A notable example of "standing in the gap" is found in the story of Moses and the Israelites. When Moses departed to Mount Sinai (where he collected the two tablets of stone of the testimony of the law), the children of Israel resorted to building a graven image, thus, breaking the law of God. The Bible records that the wrath of God was kindled against the people, but Moses stood in the gap. He made an inspiring statement that captures the heart of an intercessor:

Then Moses pleaded with the Lord his God, and said: "Lord, why does Your wrath burn hot against Your people whom You have brought out of the land of Egypt with great power and with a mighty hand? Why should the Egyptians speak and say, 'He brought them out to harm them…' Turn from Your fierce wrath, and relent from this harm to Your people. Remember Abraham,

Isaac, and Israel, Your servants by whom You swore… and said to them, "I will multiply your descendants as the stars of heaven; and all this land that I have spoken to your descendants…" (Exodus 32: 11-13)

It is interesting to see that Moses spoke as a real advocate. He gave clear and reasonable reasons for which God had to forgive the sins of the Israelite. He stood in the gap between the wrath of God and the obviously guilty Israelites. This is more evident in his words: *Yet now, if you will forgive their sin—but if not, I pray, blot me out of Your book which You have written. (Exodus 32:32)*. He obviously could relate with their troubles that he was ready to endure some suffering for them, to ensure that they are out of it.

Standing in the gap for your immediate family members, relatives, friends, church members, colleagues at work, nations, etc. is a core responsibility for any Christian woman. In the Foreword, I referred to the analogy that describes women as the 'neck' while men are the head. This analogy is mostly used within the context of marriage. Thus, it only shows the stupendous role of the woman in a family setting. Not only does the neck hold the head, it decides whatever the head sees. The turning of the head is not possible without the cooperation of the neck. In the same vein, women wield a very strong control over, not just the head of the family, but over the whole family. This control, of course, is in the place of standing in the gap through intercession.

Susanna Wesley is a notable example of a woman who had a constant life of standing in the gap. She, like many other women, was faced with challenges that would naturally make it difficult to have a prayer life. Susanna had nineteen children (out of which nine died in infancy). She was married to Samuel, who was not successful in his nearly four-decade stay as a minister of a church in a rural community. Given his unconventional and rather divisive sermons, he was hated by a greater percentage of the populace. The family were constantly subjected to all forms of insults and harassment. The family also suffered lots of financial difficulties, so much so that Samuel spent months in debtors' prison, on two occasions.

The troubles that the family had faced probably contributed to the legendary and ever-inspiring prayer life of Susanna Wesley. She had a unique method of shedding off the distractions that were likely to come from her children when it was time for prayers. She sat on her favorite chair and threw her apron over her head in such a way that it formed a sort of tent. Having gotten used to seeing this, her children came to understand what it means. When she got into that "tent," it was time to intercede for her husband and children. She stood in the gap between her husband and his constant troubles, and, also, in-between her children and their future. She dedicated about two hours of her daily life to do this.

By the time Susanna passed away in 1742, at the age of

seventy-three years, her sons John and Charles Wesley were renowned preachers who maintained her legacy of prayers and intercession. Not only was she a key influence on her family, she eventually became a fundamental influence on generations of Christians globally.

Susanna's story is one which proves that the key role that women can play in changing their families, nations, and, by extension, the world if we embrace the culture of "standing in the gap." The fact that women are naturally a lot more sensitive and emotional (compared to men) equips them with the wherewithal to fill the gap of intercessors easily. It is why it isn't so surprising that there were a handful of women in the gathering that stood in the gap for Peter's release from prison. We can build on this by choosing to stand in the gap through intercessions, instead of worrying. The letter to the Philippians puts it this way: *Be anxious for nothing, but in everything by prayer and supplication, with thanksgiving, let your request be made known unto God (Philippians 4:8).*

When people around us, like family members, relatives, friends, and neighbors, go through difficult times, there are chances that we will also be worried. However, it is important to note that the best response at times like that is to reach out to them physically, the best way we can, and, more importantly, to stand in the gap for them in intercession.

Standing in the Gap for Family, Friends, and Colleagues

"We are praying for you" is an expression that is quite common with us as Christians, when relating with people who are going through difficult times. However, while it is surely comforting to hear that someone is praying for you during your difficult times, it is more important to have them actually pray. Standing in the gap is basically about actually staying in the place of prayers for troubled people till we see the results of our prayers. Of course, there isn't anything wrong with making people know that you are praying for them. It is only important to ensure that we aren't just doing it perfunctorily if we must at all.

I have related with several women who have had something to pray about for their relatives, children, husbands or husbands-to-be, etc. This has been my experience a number of times too. Now, it is not uncommon to think these issues can be addressed just physically. While, of course, we can talk an erring relative out of making a wrong decision sometimes, this may not always be possible.

I have known Marie for many years, both in and out of the classroom. She is naturally a vibrant, smart, full-of-life and fun-to-work-with lady. She is a single mother of one: a fourteen-year-old boy. Having had her for over three years as my teaching assistant, I can say you would assume she is never vulnerable to any pressure whatsoever if you were meeting her for the first time. However, it turned out anyone would be wrong to do so. Not too long ago, I observed Marie had gradually lost her vibrancy and would often carry a worried and perplexed look on her face always. This, of course, looked strange. I was compelled to take some time off with her so we could have a chat. Then, I learned, it was about her son. He would often use swear words while communicating with her, wouldn't take her advice, and would stay away from home for long hours, hanging out with what she describes as "a dangerous-looking group of boys." This was what had begun to worry Marie.

Fortunately, I had been reading a book on prayer for almost a week before then. The book shared some powerful to insights on intercessory prayers. I shared a bit of these with Marie and got her a copy of the book. She took it upon herself to spend time in prayer for her son. Just about three weeks after, her son had become so tractable. He would listen and yield her advice this time and had stopped the use of swear words. Over the next few weeks, he changed his company, on his mother's request. Marie's son had become what exactly she had stood in the gap for him to be!

Similarly, you can stand in the gap for a troubled and/or wayward relationship partner, relative, neighbor, and etc. This requires that you plan your days or weeks to allow you dedicate ample time to prayer.

Standing in the Gap for a Nation or People

A lot of times, we hear, on the news, about nations plagued with wars, unrests, terrorism, and etc. However, we tend to do nothing, especially when our countries or that of our loved ones are not concerned. At such times, we often seem to forget that our prayers can break geographical, ideological, cultural and language barriers to cause a change. The apostle Paul was expressing this fact when he exhorted: *supplications, prayers, intercessions, and giving of thanks be made for all men, for kings and all who are in authority that we may lead a quiet and peaceable life… (1 Timothy 2:1-2).*

In the words of Edmund Burke, *the only thing necessary for the triumph of evil is for good men to do nothing.* While we may be taking actions that are expected of us socially for our nations and/or other nations and peoples, it is important that we stand in the gap for them in prayers. Even though it is not out of place to exercise our civil rights, as expected of us politically, we also have to know, as Christians, that we are not wrestling against flesh and blood (Ephesians 6:12). Hence, standing in the gap for our nations, other nations and people is a very important part of our ministry of reconciliation. As women, we are equipped with the ability to care and to stand in the gap for others in the place of prayers and intercessions.

Standing in the Gap for Persecuted Christians and Church Leaders

As Christians, we are collectively the body of Christ,

irrespective of our differences in denomination, culture, language, and etc. This means we have to live cooperatively, caring for one another. One of the ways of doing this is standing in the gap for one another. As we have earlier seen, the epistles are replete with instructions of praying for one another.

Christian persecution around the world is obviously on the rise. So many Christians have been victims of terrorism, intolerant environments, and etc. While some of us may not be experiencing the same thing wherever we are, it is important that we stand in the gap for those who are currently going through this. The epistle to Thessalonians shows that our prayers are important to the safety of persecuted lay Christians, Christian missionaries and leaders all around the world: *Finally, brethren, pray for us, that the word of the Lord may run swiftly and be glorified, just as it is with you, and that we may be delivered from unreasonable and wicked men; for not all have faith (2 Thessalonians 3:1).*

Becoming an Esther

Esther is one of the most inspiring women figures in the Bible. Her story is one that is full of so many lessons for Christian women. She was a relative to Mordecai, a Benjamite who was taken captive from Jerusalem. Esther had been brought up by Mordecai as his own child since she had no father nor mother. She became the king's wife by sheer favor in a contest of young virgins from all over the empire.

A man named Haman was promoted to the highest position at the king's court. In spite of the king's decree for all to bow before him, Mordecai refused. When the king's servants questioned him about his action, he told them he was a Jew. Eventually, when Haman learned about Mordecai's refusal to bow to him, he vowed to exterminate not only Mordecai but all Jews altogether. Haman, thus, spoke to the king, painting the Jews before him as a people who did not observe his laws, and was given the authority to carry out his wish.

Letters were published throughout to publicize the fixed date for the extermination of all Jews. Mordecai, having learned this, reached-out to Esther: *Do not think in your heart that you will escape in the king's palace any more than all the other Jews. For if you remain completely silent at this time, relief and deliverance will arise for the Jews from another place, but you and your father's house will perish (Esther 4:13-14)*. In response, Esther made the famous statement:

*Go gather all the Jews who are present in Shushan, and fast for me; neither eat nor drink for three days, night or day. My maids and I will fast likewise. **And so I will go to the king, which is against the law; and if I perish, I perish!** (Esther 4:16)*

Anyone who appears before the king without having been summoned would be put to death, according to the law, except one to whom He extended the golden scepter (Esther 4:11). Esther was, thus, undertaking what we'll call, in today's terms, "a suicide mission." She was about to embark on a task that could take her life to intercede for the Jews. When, eventually, she appeared before the king, she found favor before him. The lives of the Jews were preserved. Mordecai was made the king's chief advisor, while Haman was executed on the gallows he had prepared for Mordecai.

Becoming an Esther is about embracing the ministry of intercession with a mindset that says, *"If I perish, I perish."* Of course, it is unlikely that you are risking your life by spending time in prayers. Unlike Esther, we are surely privileged that we aren't necessarily embarking on any life-threatening risk by embracing our ministry of intercession. However, one thing we surely cannot escape is the rigor involved in taking-up our intercessory ministry the way we ought to. Our time for leisure and comfort will surely be affected, and our energies will be required. History records that Susanna Wesley vowed never to spend more time on leisure than she did on prayer. If you ask me, I think that is what it means to become an Esther.

The several people around us, both far and near, known and unknown, relatives and non-relatives, who need our prayers, are the "Jews" for which we should, like Esther, be willing to sacrifice our comforts. The tendency to feel lethargic because we aren't affected is aptly summed up in

Mordecai's words, *Do not think in your heart that you will escape in the king's palace any more than all the other Jews.* In other words, who says you'll always be safe?

By becoming an Esther, choosing to lose our comforts to intercede for others, we are simply fulfilling the words of Jesus: *For whosoever desires to save his life will lose it, but whosoever loses his life for My sake will find it (Mathew 16:25).* Like Esther, we have to shelve the pleasures of the palace and to identify with the sufferings of others. What this means, in essence, is that we have to embrace our ministry of intercession with utmost passion. Our pleasures, leisure, comfort, etc. should not get in our way. By choosing to identify with the sufferings of others around us in the place of constant prayers and intercessions, we become like Esther.

On the Wings of Influence

Our conventional understanding of what it means to be influential is to be equipped with the financial, economic, or charismatic ability to affect the behaviors of others. Even though this idea is just apt, in the sense of our daily secular activities, it tends to becloud our awareness of how much influence we wield in the place of prayers. We only tend to limit ourselves to our economic or material wherewithal.

Our ministry as intercessors puts us in a position of influence. By influence, I do not mean any form of physical or political power or authority, but a spiritual capacity to cause changes around us. Who could have thought that a gathering of a few Christians in the house of Mary, the mother of John who was also called Mark, could have overwritten the intention of Herod to kill Peter? Esther's decision to embark on an intercessory mission altered the death sentence on the lives all Jews in the Persian Empire! These are proofs of the influence that we wield, as women, when we embrace our ministry as Intercessors.

When our wings of influence are widened in the place of intercession, we have the authority to influence what goes on in our societies. Evil can only thrive when we fold our hands, doing nothing. However, by standing our ground in the place of intercession, we can spiritually alter the course of things. By embracing the ministry of intercession, your wings of influence can be spread over your family, your neighbors, societies, and all that you choose to pray about.

Now, it is important to note that our ministry of intercession does not necessarily replace our natural and physical responsibilities. We are surely required to try to address and solve problems, to the best our abilities, in the physical. However, the point is that our physical efforts cannot be relied upon without wielding our spiritual authority through the ministry of intercession.

You can embrace the ministry of intercession by earmarking specific times daily to pray about specific issues and standing in the gap for family, friends, colleagues, fellow

Christians, nations, and etc. Prepare a detailed list of the people and issues you'll like to begin to pray about. You can update this list from time to time to include new things to pray about or to replace answered prayers points.

Prayer

Dear Father, I thank You for revealing, to me, the knowledge of Your word concerning the ministry of intercession. Thank You for the privilege to serve in the place of intercession. I choose to embrace this ministry, and I declare that I will be constantly fruitful in it in the name of Jesus Christ. Amen.

A Glance through Your Bible

Psalm 122:6-9; 1 Timothy 2:1-3

Psalm 122:6 Pray for the peace of Jerusalem: May they prosper who love you. 7Peace be within your walls, prosperity within your palaces. 8For the sake of my brethren and companions, I will now say, "Peace be within you." 9Because of the house of the Lord our God, I will seek your good.

1 Timothy 2:1 Therefore I exhort first of all that supplications, prayers, intercessions, and giving of thanks be made for all men; 2for kings and all who are in authority that we may lead a quiet and peaceable life in all godliness and reverence. 3For this is good and acceptable in the sight of God our savior, who

desires all men to be saved and to come to the knowledge of the truth.

Study Questions

- How is cooperation important to the body of Christ?
- How is Christian cooperation important to the ministry of intercession?
- How does the expression, "stand in the gap," relate to intercession?
- What are the traits equip women with the special ability to better fill in the gap as intercessors, compared to men?
- How can one become an Esther in the place of intercession?
- How can we spread our wings of influence?

6

Strength from the Word

No matter how small or easy our daily activities may seem, one truth we cannot deny is the fact that we require some amount of energy to execute them. Now, when we often think of energy, we think in terms of the ability to carry out some physically demanding task. We seem to forget that even our thinking demands some significant amount of energy. Medical research proves that the brain alone consumes about twenty percent of the body's energy when it carries out its task of processing and transmitting information. Other various activities that we carry out consciously or unconsciously also place a demand on our energy. Hence, the need for a decent amount of energy in the human body is indispensable to carrying out important tasks.

Energy is formed in our bodies when we consume food. With the help of acids and enzymes in our stomach, our body digests the food we consume, works on the carbohydrate extracted, and turns it into energy. Thus, the need to consume food with the required amount of carbohydrate is often emphasized by medical professionals. Without a feeding habit that supplies our bodies with the needed energy for our daily living, chances are that we will be less effective and productive as we should be.

Just the same way our bodies require constant feeding to be supplied with the appropriate amount of energy, our spirits also require constant nourishing to keep us spiritually effective, productive, and joyful. However, unlike our body, the energy that we require for our spirits come from the word of God. Jesus expressed this fact in His response to the devil's temptation. *It is written, Man shall not live by bread alone, but by every word that proceeds from the mouth of God (Matthew 4:4).* Jesus simply pointed out that the indispensability of God's word to the human spirit, the same way physical food is to the physical body.

The tendency to feel lethargic and apathetic about prayer or consciously living and walking in the will of God is one that cannot be denied. Sometimes, we are likely to feel emotionally detached from our service to God. Such times should be expected and prepared for, as they signal a need for more strength. The prophet Isaiah captures this reality very succinctly, in his words:

Even the youths shall faint and be weary, and the young men shall utterly fall. But those that wait upon the Lord shall renew their strength; they shall mount up with wings as eagles, they shall run and not be weary, they shall walk and not faint (Isaiah 40:30-31).

Usually, after spending several hours at work, you come home a little tired and needing to freshen up, eat, and take some rest. Now, there is nothing abnormal about this, as you must have had to spend a significant amount of energy at work. Basically, for every energy-sapping task we carry out, our body naturally craves some moment to get replenished with the energy we must have lost. Now, in the same vein, we need to dedicate enough time to replenishing our spiritual energy by staying connected to the word of God.

Over the years, I have had a constant practice of ensuring that I stay connected to the word of God. I have learned, by experience, that true strength is derived from those times I spend in fellowship with and around the word. They could be times spent listening to God's word as shared by other believers and ministers of the gospel, or times spent alone studying through the Scriptures. One truth I cannot deny is the fact that I have always been instantly transformed in the place of fellowship with the word. The voice of doubts, inability and hopelessness suddenly dissipate; new inspiration, zeal and strength suddenly flood my mind. The doubt and fear that the enemy had flooded my mind with suddenly becomes clear to me as the mirage that it has always been.

Spending enough time with loved ones, doing the things

that we love to do, and etc. are helpful tips, often prescribed by psychologists, therapists, and other related professionals, to help us stay happy. While these ideas work, to some extent, the fact is that they really do not provide us with the constant joy that is independent of the situations around us. We may be disappointed by our loved ones. Even the things we love to do may soon turn out to be insufficient in keeping us happy, especially when we are faced with difficult times. But, while every other thing may fail, one thing is sure to guarantee us an eternal life of joy; it is the word of God.

So shall My word be that goes forth from My mouth; It shall not return to Me void, But it shall accomplish what I please, And it shall prosper in the thing for which I sent it. For ye shall go out with joy, and be led forth with peace… (Isaiah 55:11-12).

God's word is our surest source of strength, in a world that is filled with depression, dashed hopes, failed promises, and etc. We have to understand that we are, first of all, born of God's word. *…having been born again, not of corruptible seed but of incorruptible, through the word of God (1 Peter 1:23).* Hence, the word of God is not only a source of our strength, it is the source of our whole being. This means that whatever alternative that we subscribe to, outside of the word, wouldn't produce sufficient result for us.

Standing on God's Promises

I earlier spoke about my former teaching assistant, Marie. I must add that, asides being smart and full-of-life, she is also a naturally precise lady. Her rare ability to give reports of things exactly as they are is one of the captivating facts about her. She is naturally meticulous, plain, and truthful that I can make my conclusions based on her description of things. Now, I must say, at this point, that I am not just unnecessarily exalting Marie. I have worked with and seen tens of others work in the same capacity. Yet, I am certain that none of them quite match her at this. I am naturally careful with what I accept; I like to prove and verify things before working with them. But my experience working with Marie gave me less reason to spend too much time doing this. Now, if an imperfect human being could be so reliable, how much more a perfect God.

We have too many convincing reasons to trust in God's promises. Foremost among them is the fact that God has perfect and immaculate integrity. His truthfulness is certainly beyond our human comprehension. This is because we are imperfect, and would often tend to relate with the perfect God, from our imperfect perspective. As humans, we surely have had moments when we compromised on the truth, whether consciously or unconsciously, intentionally or accidentally. However, with God, the case is totally different. The Scriptures give us sufficient proofs for this.

God is not a man that he should lie, nor a son of man, that he should repent. Has He said, and will He not make it good (Numbers 23:19)?

And also the Strength of Israel will not lie nor relent. For He is not a man, that He should relent (1 Samuel 15:29).

In hope of eternal life which God, who cannot lie, promised before the world began… (Titus 1:2)

Since it is impossible for God to lie, standing on His promises cannot be a risky adventure. Of course, our analytic minds may give us reasons to doubt. Nevertheless, it is left to us to choose what to focus on. We can either choose to stand on His promises or to pay attention to the reasons why the promises will fail. However, to doubt His promises is to put ourselves at a disadvantage. *…for he who doubts is like a wave of the sea driven and tossed by the wind. But let not that man suppose that he will receive anything from the Lord (James 1:6-7).*

Doubt makes it difficult to walk in the promises of God. First, they make God's promises appear unreal to us. Thus, when in doubt, we are less likely to appropriate these promises into our life. Rather, we focus on the conflicting reality. The 14th chapter of Matthew tells an important story. The disciples of Jesus were stuck in the midst of the sea, on their way to Capernaum. Jesus wasn't with them, and their boat was being tossed about by a boisterous wind. They got even more terrified when they saw Jesus coming towards them walking on the sea. They thought it was a ghost! But Jesus responded immediately, *It is I. Do not be afraid (Matthew 14:27)*. In response, Peter requested, *Lord, if it is You, command me to come to You on the water (verse 25)*. Jesus obliged his request. Now, here is what follows:

...And when Peter had come down out of the boat, he walked on the water to go to Jesus. But when he saw that the wind was boisterous, he was afraid; and beginning to sink, he cried out saying, "Lord save me!" And Jesus immediately stretched out His hand and caught him, and said to him. "O you of little faith, why did you doubt?" (Matthew 14:29-31).

Peter had obviously started on the right track. He believed that Jesus' words were trustworthy, reliable and powerful enough to keep him floating on the water. Hence, he took a step of faith by walking on it. He actually walked on water for a moment. But something noteworthy happened: *when he saw that the wind was boisterous, he was afraid, and began to sink.* Of course, he knew that the wind was boisterous before he stepped into the water. He knew it was naturally impossible for a man to walk on water before he stepped into the water. He also knew that he could walk on water if Jesus asked him to (that's why he took the bold step, in the first place). Why, then, the sudden observation of the boisterousness of the wind? Bible scholars agree that Peter simply shifted his attention away from Jesus to focus on the wind.

The way to walk in faith is to keep our gaze on His promises. Peter made the costly mistake of taking his eyes off Jesus to focus on the wind. By so doing, he forgot the same words that inspired him to step into the water, in the first place: "come." Focusing his gaze on Jesus and His word (promise) was all the recipe and strategy that Peter needed to walk on water. Nevertheless, Jesus rescued him, but with the question, "why did you doubt?" I think Jesus was simply asking him, "why did you take your attention off me?"

To stand on the promises of God is to stay in faith. To look around and be distracted by the challenges that we are faced is dangerous. We must be able to say, like Edward Mote's old hymn, *On Christ the solid rock I stand. All other ground is sinking sand.* His promises should be our strongest confidence.

Paying Attention to His Promises

It will be impossible to stand on the promises of God without firstly paying our utmost attention to them. How, in the first place, do we get to learn about God's promises to us if not through the functionality of our attention? Now, it is by constantly keeping these promises in mind, we are more likely to build our stand on them. The epistle to the Roman church gives us an insight: *So then faith comes by hearing, and hearing by the word of God (Romans 10:17).* Hearing, here, may not be taken totally literal. It is used as a description for receiving, irrespective of whether you read, saw, or heard it.

Faith is birthed in when we constantly fellowship with the promises of God in the Scriptures.

Solomon, in summing up his father's advice to him, expresses the mind of God concerning how we ought to respond to His words and promises. He records his father's words thus:

My son, give attention to my words; incline your hear unto my sayings. Do not let them depart from your eyes; keep them in the midst of your heart; for they are life to those that find them, and health to all their flesh (Proverbs 4:20-22).

There are a few important details to point out in this passage. The first is the sentence: "Give attention to my words." The second is "Do not let them depart from your eyes." The third is "Keep them in the midst of your heart."

Give attention to my words: The usage of the word, attention, gives us a clue what is in the mind of David as he schooled his son, Solomon. Attention loosely means to "concentrate on." By attending to something, you are physically and mentally leaving every other thing behind to focus on it. This only proves to us that fellowshipping with God's word isn't effective when it is done passively or absentmindedly.

Often times, we may be tempted to read through and study God's word perfunctorily. This happens when we try to read through some Christian books, just out of peer pressure; or trying to study our Bible, just to stick to every item on our timetable. Even though these aren't exactly bad, there is need to go beyond "just doing it" to "really doing it." We have to know why we do what we do. We have to be aware of the stupendous importance of studying through God's word.

It is in the conscious act of studying through fellowshipping with His word that we are able to learn about and stand on His promises. This is where our faith is built. It is where we derive the strength and joy that keeps us living our life to the full. It is where we derive true fulfillment that is beyond words.

Do not let them depart from your eyes: Even though it may be impossible to keep your eyes constantly on a book, the message, here, is quite clear. The "eyes" are aptly described as the windows through which we communicate with our immediate surroundings or environment. Now, to never allow God's word to depart from that "window" would mean to relate with our immediate environment from the perspective of God's word. In other words, God's word alone would determine what we choose to see or not see. This means we will only choose to see things that are in congruence with His promises, and refuse to pay our attention to anything that contradicts His promise.

Keep them in the midst of your heart: By keeping the word "in the midst of your heart," you simply allow it to sink into your innermost being. Now, the way to doing this is by allowing it in our minds first, and then cultivating a culture of meditating on it.

The Need for Meditation

When Moses died, Joshua became saddled with the task of leading the children of Israel to the Promised Land. At this point, the Lord spoke to him, and encouraged him to be strong and courageous. Among other instructions, the Lord pointed out the need for constant meditation to him. His success and prosperity would, in fact, depend on how much meditation he did.

This book of the law shall not depart from your mouth, but you shall meditate in it day and night, that you may observe to do according to all that is written in it. For then, you will make your way prosperous, and have good success (Joshua 1:8).

The instruction to Joshua seems to suggest that the capacity to carry out corresponding actions of faith will be dependent on how much we meditate on His word. Meditation imparts faith into our spirits, thus equipping us with the capacity to stand firm and unshaken on the promises of God.

Over the years, I have cultivated a culture of constant meditation on God's word, especially on areas that contain His promises for us. One thing this does is that it helps dispel doubts and fears. You can practice a steady culture of meditating on God's word daily, especially during periods you may be prone to discouraging thoughts. This would literally help you replace those thoughts of inability, fear, etc. with thoughts of God's promises for you. Now, the more you meditate, the more real these promises become. This is why the amount of time we spend meditating plays an important role.

The beautiful thing about meditating is that you do not necessarily need to read through any material to do it. You also may not need to leave whatever you are doing behind before you are able to meditate. The word "meditate," as used in Joshua, was translated from the Hebrew word, *"hagah"* which means to ponder. This means to think about something intensely. This often requires speaking or muttering it to yourself. This explains why the text reads "… *shall not depart out of your mouth."*

Now, to meditate on God's word means to think upon the Scriptures, particularly what they say about us. When we meditate, we mentally appropriate the promises of God, found in His word, to our lives. For instance, if you are faced with thoughts of being lonely and abandoned, portions of Scriptures like the following might just be apt: *Yea, though I walk through the valley of the shadow of death, I will fear no evil; for You are with me; Your rod and Your staff, they comfort me (Psalm 23:4). …For He Himself has said, "I will never leave you nor forsake you." So that we may boldly say: "The Lord is my Helper. I will not fear. What can man do to me?" (Hebrews 13:5).*

...Lo, I am with You always, even to the end of the age (Matthew 28:20).

It is important to note that whatever we require is available in God's word. All that we have to do is to locate these promises in His word and to dedicate our time to meditate on them. Simply think upon, mutter and speak the promises to yourself. If, for instance, you are faced with thoughts of fear on your abilities, you can simply say, like the apostle Paul, "I can do all things through Christ who strengthens me" (Philippians 4:13). However, meditation goes beyond just saying it absentmindedly; your attention must be involved. Your imagination also has a role to play. While meditating on those words, create corresponding pictures in your mind.

If you dedicate enough time to meditate on the promises of God, it surely won't take time before you begin to experience noteworthy results. Meditate upon these things; give yourself entirely to them, that your progress may be evident to all (1 Timothy 4:15).

In the Face of Turbulences

In our daily walk, the tendency to experience challenges that "attack" our faith is one that is quite common. These challenges may come in the form of financial difficulties, career or job-related problems, battered relationships, and etc. At such dark and lonely moments, you are likely to be less concerned about fulfilling the will of God. Such trying times seem to take hold of your attention, causing you to be less interested in the things of God. However, it is always up to you to choose your response.

Having been faced with some intensely difficult moments, I understand how difficult these times are. At such difficult times, you feel like the whole world is against you. This feeling is made even worse when families or loved ones turn their backs against you when depressing thoughts flood your mind, and everything seems just bleak.

Times of trials and turbulences are bound to come from time to time. If they don't come from our secular life, they'll definitely come from persecutions against us as Christian women. Now, God did not promise us a life that is free from challenges, however, He promised never to abandon us at such times. Jesus said: *These things I have spoken to you, that in Me you may have peace. In the world, you will have tribulations; but be of good cheer, I have overcome the world (John 16:33).* While tribulations may come from time to time, one very sure fact is that we will have peace in Christ. By simply putting our trust in Him, trusting that He is with us, we will surely experience that inner tranquility that surpasses every other thing.

The lie that the enemy tries to bring to us is that God abandons us at times of trouble. What this does to us, if we accept it, is to make us unable to recognize His presence. By not accepting His presence, we will be unable to rest in His love, and to fellowship with Him. One thing God wants us to know is that He is with us all through our difficult times. He doesn't abandon us at any point in time. The prophet Isaiah captures the mind of God very plainly:

When you pass through the waters, I will be with you; and through the rivers, they shall not overflow you. When you walk through the fire, you shall not be burned, nor any flame scorch you (Isaiah 43:2).

One thing we easily note in Isaiah's words is the fact that God doesn't tell us we will not pass through the waters and fire. However, He does promise us that He will not leave us; He will be with us through these difficult times. This brings to mind the story in Daniel Chapter 3, of the three young men of Israel who were captured to Babylon. King Nebuchadnezzar had set up an image, to which he expected all the officers of the province to worship and bow to. However, Shadrach, Meshach and Abednego resolved in their heart that they would not bow. This was against the law of their God. When the king learned about their defiance of his authority, he threatened to cast them in the midst of a fiery furnace, and he meant it. But, the three young men were not willing to compromise; they maintained their stance thus:

O Nebuchadnezzar, we have no need to answer you in this matter. If that is the case, our God whom we serve is able to deliver us from the burning fiery furnace, and He will deliver us from your hand, O King (Daniel 3:16-17).

Somehow, they didn't let the intense heat from the furnace deter them. They were firm and resolute with their convictions. In fact, chances are that they refused to pay attention to the furnace, but to the fact that God is able to deliver them. The king became much more enraged at their words and demanded that the furnace be heated up seven times more. He then commanded the three young men to be bound and thrown into the fire. Even the men who threw them into the fire were killed by the intense heat from the flame; but, guess what, the three young men were delivered supernaturally. A fourth man appeared in the fire with them! Nebuchadnezzar, obviously alarmed, described this thus: *I see four men loose, walking in the midst of the fire, and they are not hurt, and the form of the fourth is like the Son of God (Daniel 3::25).*

Looking at the story of the three young Israelites, we see the demonstration of God's deliverance in times of trouble. While being bound, in preparation to be thrown into the intense fire, Shadrach, Meshach, and Abednego could have wondered, for a moment, "wouldn't God do something now?" However, they refused to consider the fiery furnace. They understood that God was able to deliver them, even in the midst of the furnace.

We are expected to take actions of faith similar to that of Shadrach, Meshach, and Abednego. This can be done by our refusal to acknowledge the turbulence or the "fiery furnace" close to us. We have to trust Him to be with us even from the midst of the fiery furnace. Thus, the fire would surely have no effect on us. It is important that we choose not to forget the promise of God. Jesus said: *I will not leave you as orphans; I will come to you. A little while longer and the world will see me no more, but you will see Me. Because I live, you will live also (John 14:18-19).*

While We Do Not Look…

For our light affliction, which is but for a moment, is working for us a far more weight of eternal glory, while we look not at the things which are seen, but at the things which are not seen. For the things which are seen are temporary, but the things which are not seen are eternal (2 Corinthians 4:17-18).

The above passage is one of the most inspiring counsels for Christians going through periods of tribulations. The first thing the spirit of God, through the apostle Paul, points out is the fact that our afflictions, no matter how intense they may feel, are light. They are light! Yes, and that's because they are for a moment. To let the tribulations that we are faced with get to rob will be to cheat ourselves of some joy. These tribulations wouldn't last; they are for a moment. Now, how do we walk in joy and live our lives to the full even in the midst of these tribulations? The answer is to simply refuse to acknowledge that which is seen for that which is unseen. That which is unseen stands for His promises to us. All other things will pass away, but His promises to us will never fail to come to pass.

Choosing not to look at the wind was all that Peter required to have walked on water just as Jesus did. Similarly, choosing not to look at the turbulences (the things which are seen), but to focus on His promises (the things which are not seen) is just the perfect recipe to walking through the fire, like Shadrach, Meshach, and Abednego. Remember Jesus guaranteed us joy only in Him: *These things I have spoken to you, that in Me you may have peace. In the world, you will have tribulations (John 16:33).* In other words, our joy is in acknowledging the promises that we have in Him. When we pay our attention to the tribulations around us, we aren't dwelling in Him. To dwell in Him is to focus on Him and His promises. This is where we definitely find peace. The apostle James helps us see one of the ways to do this:

My brethren, count it all joy when you fall into various trials, knowing that the testing of your faith produces patience. But let patience have its perfect work, that you may be perfect and complete, lacking nothing (James 1:2-4).

The lesson here is the need to count our trials and tribulations "all joy." This is done by, first of all, knowing! The knowing proves to be the most fundamental response. We have to know God's promises to us. James describes these periods as just a mere "testing" of our faith, which produces patience. In other words, it is only for a moment.

Times of tribulations should be faced with a knowing of the promises of God to us. This "knowing" isn't just mere head knowledge of what the Scriptures say, but a deep-seated acknowledgement of His promises for us. This means we do not only have to know these promises, but also have to meditate on them, and include them in our daily lives. They should dominate our prayers, thoughts, speech, and etc. By refusing to pay our attention to the tribulations around and choosing rather to look at that which is unseen (God's promises for us), we are constantly supplied with all the strength we require to live happy, joyful and fulfilled, irrespective of the challenges around.

Prayer

Dear Father, I know that You love me and want the best for me. I choose to always acknowledge Your love, provisions and promises for me. I refuse to allow tribulations to dictate my fellowship with You. I refuse to allow depressing and destructive thoughts to take hold of my mind. I choose to always yield myself to the joy, peace, and love that is found in Your spirit in me. Amen.

A Glance through Your Bible

Isaiah 40:29-31; 2 Peter 1:4-6

Isaiah 40:29 He gives power to the weak, and those who have

no might He increases strength. ³⁰Even the youths shall faint and be weary, and the young men shall utterly fall, ³¹But those who wait upon the Lord shall renew their strength; they shall mount up with wings as eagles, they shall run and not be weary, they shall walk and not faint.

---

2 Peter 1:4-6 By which have been given to us exceedingly great and precious promises, that through these, you may be partakers of the divine nature, having escaped the corruption that is in the world through lust. ⁵But for this reason, giving all diligence, add to your faith virtue, to virtue knowledge, ⁶to knowledge self-control, to self-control perseverance, to perseverance godliness.

Study Questions

- Why do we require "energy" for our spirits?
- What are some signs that help us know if we are weak in the spirit?
- Why should we put our trust in God's promises?
- Why is it dangerous to doubt the promises of God for us?
- What lessons can we learn from Peter's encounter with Jesus on the sea?
- Why is meditation important?
- How do we maintain faith in the midst of trials and turbulences?

7

The Deborah Anointing

Through history, women have played key leadership roles, even in the most chauvinistic societies. The story of Deborah is a very apt example of this. She was one of the "judges" of the people of Israel, sent to deliver them from their enemies. Now, this was the period after Joshua's death. The Bible records that, during this period, *the Lord raised up judges who delivered them out of the hands of those who plundered them (Judges 2:16)*. Deborah's position as one of the most notable of these Judges is clear proof that women can be massive tools in the hands of God if we avail ourselves to be used of Him. The "Deborah anointing" is one with which each and every one of us can also function.

Before Deborah came into the picture, the Israelites had experienced the leadership of three judges who each judged and delivered them from the oppression of some other nation. The first of them was Othniel, who delivered them from their eight-year servitude to the king of Mesopotamia.

When Othniel died, Ehud delivered them from the dominion of Eglon, king of Moab. Ehud's exploits helped them stay free from oppression for eighty years. After Ehud, Shamgar also saved them from the Philistines. The activities of these previous judges helped the children of Israel enjoy some peace until they fell into the hands of Jabin, the king of Canaan. Jabin took over the sovereignty of the children of Israel and oppressed them. Having suffered much hardship in the hands of Jabin, they prayed to God for deliverance, and God gave them Deborah.

Deborah, the wife of Lapidoth, was not only a Judge to Israel, she was also a prophetess. As a judge, the Bible records that *she would sit under the palm tree… and the children of Israel came up to her for judgment (Judges 4:5)*. She provided leadership to the people, serving in the capacity of a judge and a prophet simultaneously. She inspired the freedom of the Israelites from the hands of Jabin. Her role as a prophetess and judge was instrumental to this. The Bible records that she sent for Barak, the son of Abinoam, prophesying to him, *Has not the Lord God of Israel commanded, Go deploy troops at Mount Tabor; take with you ten thousand men…? I will deploy Sisera, the commander of Jabin's army…, and I will deliver him into your hand (Judges 4:6-7)*. Barak, thus, requested that she goes with him, and she did. With her leadership, he recruited ten thousand men.

Having gotten reports about Barak's activities, Sisera,

king Jabin's army commander, gathered his army and "nine hundred chariots of iron" in preparation for war. But Deborah, yet again, stirred up Barak with her words, *Up! For this is the day in which the Lord has delivered Sisera into your hand (Judges 4:14).* This was all that Barak and his troops needed to defeat Jabin, king of Canaan, and his army commander.

And the Lord routed Sisera and all his chariots and all his army with the edge of the sword before Barak… So on that day, God subdued Jabin, king of Canaan in the presence of the children of Israel. And the hand of the children of Israel grew stronger and stronger… until they had destroyed Jabin, king of Canaan (Judges 4:15, 23-24).

An Ideal Example of Spiritual Guidance and Leadership

One of the most notable highlights of Deborah's story is her position, not only as a judge but also as a spiritual guide. Unlike the other judges before and after her, Deborah stood out for, not only the fact that she was an amalgam of a judge and a prophetess but for her office as a guide. The Bible records that she had a practice of sitting under "the palm tree of Deborah" to judge the people (Judges 4:5). This only shows that she had a literal office and practice of providing guidance to the people of Israel. The fact that she was a prophetess surely made this possible. Now, being a prophetess meant that she was equipped with the ability to hear from God on behalf of the people.

The eventual freedom of the people of Israel from Jabin, the king of Canaan, couldn't have been possible without the prophetic gift of Deborah. Jabin had a military advantage that is specifically identified in the Bible: *And the children of Israel cried out to the Lord, for Jabin had nine hundred chariots of iron… (Judges 4:3).* The possession of such military equipment by Jabin meant that it was impossible, from the natural perspective, for Israel to overcome him. The fact that king Jabin also had a real army (led by Sisera) further establishes how logically unfeasible it was for Israel to think about going into a battle against them. However, Deborah's prophetic gift proved just invaluable. Her insights into God's plan and strategy for overcoming the enemy and freeing the people of Israel was what saved the day.

By virtue of her insight into God's plan for delivering the Israelites, Deborah identified Barak as the man for the job. She also identified the exact strategy from God: *Go and deploy troops at Mount Tabor; take with you ten thousand men of the sons of Naphtali and the sons of Zebulun… (Judges 4:6).* This was just the "military strength" that Israel required. If they were to go by their natural abilities, Siseria and his army would have had a field day repelling their attack and destroying them. Israel couldn't afford to go with a plan that wasn't sure to be the perfect plan. They certainly couldn't afford to take a risk.

Thus, they found just the ideal leader in Deborah. Her ability to know the perfect supernatural strategy, and the firmness with which she stuck to it, as well as her capacity to inspire Barak and the armies to do the impossible, was astounding.

Barak, upon hearing the plan of God for him to lead the assault on the enemies, must have been quite shaken. He knew that Sisera had a huge army and nine hundred chariots of iron (which was a huge military advantage at that time). He understood that they were at a military disadvantage from all natural points of view. This definitely explains why he was quick to request of Deborah: *If you will go with me, then I will go; but if you will not go with me, I will not go (Judges 4:8).* Deborah was obviously the inspiration behind the attempt. It was a naturally impossible mission that required a leader and guide who understood that it was not by power nor might but by God's spirit (Zechariah 4:6). This was what Deborah stood for. With her around, Barak and his ten thousand men could draw inspiration to fight for their cause, knowing that God was with them.

Even though Barak and his men fought and were successful against Sisera and his armies, thus freeing the people of Israel from king Jabin, Deborah was the force behind their exploits. When Sisera rallied his nine hundred chariots of iron, I can picture how intimidated Barak was likely to have been. But Deborah was extraordinarily courageous, firm and solid. Taking her place as the real "army commander," she commanded Barak, *Up! For this is the day in which the Lord has delivered Sisera into your hand. Has not the Lord gone out before you?* This was the defining moment. They found the battle easy just as Deborah had prophesied, an evidence that they had been helped supernaturally.

Serving as a Deborah in Our Days

Deborah's story is definitely one of the most outstanding leadership stories ever told. It paints a picture of what it simply means to be a committed and inspirational leader, making it just suitable for both male and female across different ages, cultures, languages, and social settings. More importantly, Deborah's story is a very lucid biblical evidence that women can effectively serve in the place of leadership and be mightily used of God to provide deliverance to others.

Deborah grew in a society where it was unlikely for a female to lead. Before her, Israel never had a history of any woman occupying a key leadership position. It appears that most women of her times only played second fiddle to men when it came to taking social responsibilities. Thus, they probably made themselves less available to be used of God in the place of leadership. Israel, before Deborah, had only known leaders like Moses, Aaron, Joshua, and Caleb. The judges that came before her, Othniel, Ehud, and Shamger, were all men. Actually, every judge, recorded in the book of Judges, to have led Israel were all men. Deborah's exploits, nevertheless, prove that God is ever willing to make use of women when we make ourselves available to Him. The apostle Paul also gives us reason to believe that God has no bias for any gender when it comes to who to use.

There is neither Jew nor Greek, there is neither slave nor free, there is neither male nor female; for you are all one in Christ Jesus (Galatians 3:28).

The Bible helps us see that Deborah, like many other women of her days, was married. Now, this means she definitely must have had to live with the daily responsibilities that were required of her as a wife. Even though there is no biblical record for whether or not she had a child (or children), there are chances that she did. Hence, I think, we have every reason to believe that Deborah is just the regular day-to-day woman. The Bible gives us no reason to believe that she was any different from other women of her times in Israel. If any difference at all, it must have been the fact that she was equipped, by God, to be a prophetess and a judge to Israel. This, however, had to have been preceded by a life totally yielded to God's will, and a passion to serve Him.

It is important to point out that not every one of us will serve as a leader at a capacity related to that of Deborah. Nevertheless, we are equipped to cause changes in different capacities. Serving as a Deborah may not necessarily entail being a judge or a prophetess as the biblical Deborah was. It also may not be about leading any form of revolt or political movement. However, it is about being a source of influence to people around you. The biblical Deborah was, first of all, a real judge; to whom Israelites came to settle disputes. Her insights into the will and counsel of God definitely had a key role to play in this. Similarly, a contemporary Deborah can be well equipped enough to provide spiritual guidance to people around her.

It is noteworthy that everyone isn't called by God to be a church or a religious leader; however, God's plan is for all Christians to play important roles in the work of the ministry. The epistle to the Ephesian church helps us see this: *And He Himself gave some to be apostles, some prophets, some evangelists, and some pastors and teachers, **for the perfecting of the saints for the work of the ministry**... (Ephesians 4:11-12)*. Apostle Paul's instruction to Timothy makes this even clearer: *You have heard me teach things that have been confirmed by many reliable witnesses. Now, teach these truths to other trustworthy people **who will be able to pass them on to others** (1 Timothy 2:2 New Living Translation)*. This helps us see that we can serve effectively in the place of teaching and inspiring others, or guiding and adding value to them in some way. Priscilla and her husband, Aquila's encounter with Apollos helps us see how we can do this:

Now a certain Jew named Apollos, born at Alexandria, an eloquent man and mighty in scriptures came to Ephesus. This man had been instructed in the way of the Lord; and being fervent in the spirit, he spoke and taught accurately the things of the Lord, though he knew only the baptism of John. So he began to speak boldly in the synagogue. When Aquila and Priscilla heard him, they took him aside and explained to him the way of God more accurately (Acts 18:24-27).

Serving as a Deborah in our world means providing guidance to those around us. However, this comes through a conscious attempt of committing oneself to fellowshipping with God. Being a prophetess (one who speaks for God), the biblical Deborah surely must have had a life of constant fellowship with God. How else could she have learned about God's plan for freeing the people of Israel from king Jabin? How, in the first place, could she have been a prophetess and a judge, if she wasn't constantly in communion with God? Similarly, we can constantly fellowship with God through His word in order to be of help to others. Fellowshipping in the place of learning God's word is to avail ourselves to His will and purpose for our lives and that of others. Knowing this puts us in the ideal position to speak to others on God's behalf. The apostle Paul lets us see this in his words, *Let the word of Christ dwell in you richly in all wisdom, teaching and admonishing one another... (Colossians 3:16).*

Your service as a Deborah needn't be confined to any specific group or class of people. In this context, your "people of Israel" may be regular people that you have contact with on a regular basis. They could be family members, neighbors, colleagues at work, people that you interact with via online platforms, and etc. Just the same way the people of Israel saw Deborah as one to whom they could go to for spiritual guidance, you can build such legacy everywhere you find yourself. You can start with your family, particularly your kids. Timothy's mother and grandmother, for instance, happened to have greatly influenced him. Apostle Paul helps us see this in his letter to him, …*when I call to remembrance the genuine faith that is in you, which dwelt first in your grandmother, Lois, and your mother, Eunice, and I am persuaded that in you also (2 Timothy 1:5).*

Several years ago, while studying the story of Deborah and that of other inspiring women in the Bible, I realized that I could also be an answer to the prayers of others. This simply changed my thinking. I began to pay more attention to the needs of others around and thought about how to meet them. Thus, there were several times I go to God's word to find answers to the questions on the minds of many who, I believed, God brought my way. At other times, I have had to stay in the place of prayers to help deliver other people from the problems that plagued them. Amazingly, over the years, I have found so much fulfilment doing this, and that doing this had always been God's will for me. Today, with much more platforms and bigger opportunities, I have not deviated from the simple task of serving as a Deborah, who communicates the mind of God to others and provides answers to their questions. This book is one of the several means to this specific end.

Over the years, I have met several other women who could be the Deborah to their families, neighborhoods and societies. However, they have succumbed to the pressures of and distractions around them. Some were raised in religious circles, families or societies where the capacity of the woman is suppressed. Several more were not sure that they had anything to offer. Perhaps, you belong to any of these categories; all you need to know is that God knows what's best for you. He is the one who has made and fashioned you. By yielding yourself to be used by Him, you can be sure He'll take care of all that concerns you. Begin by giving yourself to fellowship with God through His word and through prayers. You can do this through constant fellowship with other like-minded believers and ministers of the gospel of Jesus Christ. Relevant and trust-worthy reading materials will also come in handy. The knowledge of God's word will bring you into the clarity of what God's exact purpose is for you, and how He wants you to serve as a Deborah per time.

Functioning with the Deborah Anointing

What is the Deborah Anointing?

Thinking about Deborah as a prophetess and a judge, you

may be quick to assume that the Deborah Anointing meant some prophetic gift or some grace for excellent judgment. Well, while these aren't necessarily out of place, the Deborah Anointing refers to something of a broader scope. I must say it is possible to be equipped with the gift of prophecy and good judgment without necessarily functioning with the Deborah Anointing. On the other hand, functioning with the Deborah Anointing may not require the gift of prophecy and the ability to judge cases. The Deborah Anointing, in this context, stands for the supernatural ability to bring deliverance to others; it is the divine capacity to provide effective and inspirational leadership. Note that the key point here is the fact that it is supernatural and divine.

I have always stood with the fact that every woman has the capacity to function with the Deborah Anointing. Irrespective of race, society, and background, any Christian woman can be used to meet needs supernaturally. It is granted that we may not function at the same capacity or level; nevertheless, every one of us can be supernatural saviors to our spheres of contact. We can be custodians of the divine power of God to change lives.

Note that functioning with the Deborah Anointing isn't the same as serving as a Deborah, even though these two may seem identical. While serving as a Deborah is about yielding ourselves to be used of God, functioning with the Deborah Anointing is about serving with the fullness of God's power.

Of course, yielding yourself to the service of God means you are able to function with God's power, at least, to a reasonable extent. However, functioning with the Deborah Anointing means giving yourself to be a custodian of the power of God to minister to others.

It is important also to note that the Deborah Anointing is only a coinage I have chosen to use to help us see that we can function supernaturally just as Deborah did. The Deborah Anointing doesn't refer to any specific kind of power that is different from God's power in and upon us in the New Testament. Rather, it refers to how we use the power of God upon us to cause similar changes to that of Deborah.

The Demonstration of Power

The need for the demonstration of God's power is fundamental to our walk if we will effectively serve as a Deborah in our world. When the Lord Jesus delivered His first sermon, the general observation of His audience was that there was something unique about Him: *And so it was, when Jesus had ended these sayings, that the people were astonished at His teaching, for He taught them as one having* **authority***, and not as the scribes (Matthew 7:28-29).* Note that the word translated authority in there is the Greek word, *"exousia,"* which primarily means power. Also, we observe that Jesus wouldn't have the apostles go into the streets to herald the news of His resurrection until they had received power. Luke helps us see this in his gospel and in his record of the Acts of the Apostles:

Then He said unto them, "Thus it is written, and thus it was necessary for the Christ to suffer and to rise from the dead the third day, and that repentance and remission of sins should be preached in His name… And you are witnesses of these things… but tarry in the city of Jerusalem until you are endued with power from on high (Luke 24: 46-49)

But you shall receive power when the Holy Spirit has come upon you; and you shall be witnesses to Me in Jerusalem, and in Judea and Samaria, and to the end of the earth (Acts 1:8)

For the Lord Jesus to have laid so much emphasis on power, and instructing the disciples to wait in Jerusalem to be endued with power, it appears that it is of utmost importance. There is every reason to believe that if the apostles had gone about the work of the ministry without waiting to be filled with power, they wouldn't have just been as effective. Surely, they had witnessed the resurrected Lord for forty days, they also witnessed many infallible proofs which convinced them that it was truly the Lord. Luke records: *…to whom He also presented Himself alive after His suffering by many infallible proofs, being seen of them forty days, and speaking of the things pertaining to the things of the kingdom of God (Acts 1:3).* I can understand that the apostles must have been eager to go all out to witness the resurrection of Christ. After all, they are now convinced about His resurrection; they had also been taught about the things of the kingdom for forty days. They had something that they felt the whole world needs to hear about. Yet, Jesus instructed them to wait till they are endued with power.

Jesus helps us see how much important it was to function with the power of God in the work of the ministry. The apostle even gives us more evidence in his epistle to the Corinthian church: *And my speech and my preaching were not with the persuasive words of human wisdom, but in demonstration of the Spirit and of power, that your faith should not stand in the wisdom of men, but in the power of God (1 Corinthians 2:4-5).* The epistle to the Thessalonian church further shows his thought: *For our gospel did not come to you in word only, but also in power (1 Thessalonians 1:5).* Apostle Paul was evidently aware of the emphasis that Jesus placed on power when he spoke with the earlier apostles. Paul knew that any sermon from human wisdom, without a clear demonstration of the power of God's spirit, would affect the faith of his hearers. With powerless sermons, the apostle Paul understood that he wouldn't make much impact. This is the same perspective that should influence our service to God.

Serving as a Deborah with the demonstration of the power of God is definitely not the same as going about it with sheer human abilities. First, we understand that the biblical Deborah had the power of God upon her life. This, of course, is what enabled her to function in the capacity of a judge and a prophetess. Now, the interesting thing is that we, as Christians, also have the spirit and power of God upon our lives. The same spirit and power that Jesus promised the apostles is also resident within us. In Acts Chapter 1, Jesus promised that the apostles would receive power after the Holy Spirit came upon them. Later on, in Chapter 2, we find out that this promise was not confined to only the apostles or to those around those times: *Then Peter said to them, repent and let every one of you be baptized in the name of Jesus Christ for the remission of sins; and you shall receive the gift of the Holy Spirit. For the promise is to you and to your children, and to all who are afar off, as many as the Lord our God will call (Acts 2:38-39).*

The epistle to the Ephesians even makes it clearer to us that anyone who has believed in the gospel of the Lord Jesus receives the same Holy Spirit: *In Him you also trusted, after you heard the word of truth, the gospel of your salvation; in whom also, having believed, you were sealed with the Holy Spirit of promise (Ephesians 1:13).* You know what this means, we are equipped with the power of God! The epistle to Timothy lets us see this: *...for God has not given us a spirit of fear, but of power... (2 Timothy 1:7).* In other words, we are supplied with power already. We do not have to wish or hope to have the kind of power upon Deborah, we have all that we require to do even greater things than she did.

While we have the power of God within us to function

effectively as "Deborahs" to our world, it is important to note that the mere knowledge of the power of God within is not enough. We have to know how to make use of the power. The Bible speaks about being strong in the Lord and in the power of His might (Ephesians 6:10). This gives us reason to believe it is possible not to take advantage of the power of God within us. How then do we take advantage of this immense power within us?

In his brief description, James lets us see an interesting function of prayer: *...the earnest prayer of a righteous person has great power and produces wonderful results (James 5:16 New Living Translation)*. This short and precise expression simply helps us see a key way of expressing the power in us. Now, not only do we pray to cause changes in some specific area, but we also pray to stir ourselves up. The apostle Paul expresses this, in his letter to Timothy, *therefore I remind you to stir up the gift of God which is in you... (2 Timothy 1:6)*. The best terms to describe what he appears to be expressing here are: activate, switch-on, rouse up, and etc. This means, while the power is constantly in us, there is need to stir it up for use.

The fundamental way of stirring up the power of God in us is through prayer. We must understand that prayer is not always about asking for things. It is primarily about fellowship with God. And when we fellowship with God in the place of prayer long enough, we have His power in us stirred up for use. The effect of Moses' encounter with God on Mount Sinai gives a brief description of this. In Exodus 34:29-31, having spent forty days and nights on the mountain with the Lord, the skin on Moses' face glowed so much that the people were afraid to come near him. The Twelve Apostles understood the role of prayer so much so that they were prepared to live every form of distraction behind. They declared: *...but we will give ourselves continually to prayer and to the ministry of the word (Acts 6:4).* Prayer was of so much importance to them that it came even before their responsibility of teaching the word.

Earlier in Acts Chapter 3, Peter and John supernaturally healed a lame man and seized the opportunity to preach to the marveled crowd who gathered as a result of the miracle. They were soon arrested by the elders at Jerusalem. These elders seriously threatened and prohibited them from preaching the gospel. In response to the persecution and threats, Peter and John returned to the company of the other apostles and recounted their experience. The apostles prayed together, and the result was: *...when they had prayed, the place where they were assembled together was shaken; and they were all filled with the Holy Spirit, and they spoke the word of God with boldness (Acts 4:31).* Note that this was after they had already received Holy Spirit that Jesus earlier promised them. Here, their encounter was somewhat a stirring-up of what they already had. No wonder they resorted to giving themselves "continually" to prayer.

Timothy was instructed to "stir-up" the gift of God in him. The apostles spoke about giving themselves "continually" to prayer. Paul wrote to the Thessalonians, *pray without ceasing… Do not quench the Spirit (1 Thessalonians 5:17, 19)*. It is our choice to function with the Deborah Anointing within us. By living a life of prayer, you and I can constantly stir-up and activate this anointing within us at every moment of our lives. By doing this, not only would you find it easier to serve God as the Deborah to your world, you will be able to live a life of richer and more tangible fellowship with God.

Prayer

Dear Father, I choose to yield myself constantly to be used by You to meet the needs of others. I choose to be the means through which You will answer the prayers of others. Henceforth, I choose to live a life of rich fellowship with You through Your word and prayers. Amen.

A Glance through Your Bible

Zechariah 4:6; 2 Psalm 68:11 (Amplified Version)

Zechariah 4:6 He answered and said unto me: "This is the word of the Lord unto Zerubbabel: Not by might nor by power, but by My spirit," says the Lord of Hosts.

____

____

2 Peter 1:4-6 The Lord gives the command; the women who proclaim the good news are a great host.

Study Questions

- How was Deborah significant to the deliverance of the people of Israel from king Jabin?
- How did Debora inspire Barak and his men to overcome Sisera and his army?
- How can one serve as a Deborah in our days?
- What does serving as a Deborah entail?
- What is the qualification for serving as a Deborah in our days?
- What does it mean to function with the Deborah anointing?
- What is the role of prayer in helping us function with the Deborah anointing?

8

Women and Ambition

As a younger woman, one of the major challenges I experienced was how to find the balance between my career, personal ambitions and the will of God for me and my family. There were periods of "clashes," when what I wanted appeared not to be the perfect thing to do. A few times, I have had to sacrifice some career achievements to do what I sensed is the perfect thing to do. Well, I must admit that such decisions are very difficult, and we may easily confuse our desires for God's will.

One of my college friends, Kim, is currently married with three beautiful kids, two boys and one girl. She is married to James, an African-American doctor. Their marriage has been just calm and peaceful for over fifteen years now. However, their first few months together was not so much fun. Kim had just gotten her dream job in another state, which was about eight hours drive from the couple's place of residence. The temptation to relocate put her marriage under much stress, for the first few months. Even though James was concerned and very understanding of her wife's dilemma, his hands were tied. He worked, at that time, in a nearby hospital, where he actually started his career. Prior to that time, they both never had the plan of relocating.

When Kim related her dilemma to me, it didn't take much time for me to realize that she was just ambitious. Of course, she loved her husband and wanted a beautiful marriage. However, she didn't want to miss the "massive" opportunity opened to her. She surely understood that any attempt to opt for the job at that location would put her marriage at risk. She had to choose which mattered to her from the two options she was faced with. Speaking with her, I expressed the need to align her desires with God's will. We spent just about 40 minutes speaking about this over a meal at her place. When we were done, she heaved a sigh of relief. It was now easy to decide not to let her ambitions overcome her love for her marriage. This is what any wife or husband will do, walking in the will of God.

Now, we have to understand that there is absolutely nothing wrong with being ambitious in our careers, jobs, business, or whatever we do. However, the problem is in letting our personal ambitions clash with the will of God for us. I explained, in Chapter 4, that the will of God for us refers to His divine desires and plans for our conducts and lives. Whatever ambition that wouldn't let us walk in love towards others, for instance, is not in consonance with the will of God. Similarly, any ambition that would take us away from our ministry and service to others is definitely one that isn't healthy. This means that all of our ambitions and desires must be in perfect sync with what God would have us do.

The tendency to get ambitious in a way that clashes with the will of God often starts from our thinking. This is why the Bible says a lot about our mind. Proverbs says, *keep your heart with all diligence, for out of it are the issues of life (Proverbs 4:23)*. Now, in context, we understand that "heart," as used here refers to the mind, where our thoughts come from. Another portion of the same book makes it even a lot clearer: *For as he thinks in his heart, so is he (Proverbs 23:7)*. Our minds determine a lot about us; particularly, it determines how we deal with our ambitions with respect to the will of God. Hence, to constantly make our ambitions align with God's will, it is necessary to mind what thoughts we accommodate. The epistle to the Romans clearly teaches us how to do this:

*...and do not be conformed to the world, but be transformed by the renewing of your mind, that you may prove what is that good, and acceptable, and perfect will of God. For I say through the grace given unto me to everyone that is among you, **not to think of himself more highly than he ought to think, but to think soberly**... (Romans 12:2-3)*

Without careful observation, we are likely to assume that the Scripture verse above is telling us not to think highly of ourselves at all. But that would be totally wrong. The Scriptures clearly teach that God has empowered, strengthened and exalted us. Paul, for instance, declared he can do all things through Christ who strengthens him (Philippians 4:13). Well, isn't it obvious that he was thinking highly of himself? The Philippian Christians were admonished to think and meditate on things that are praiseworthy, of good report, etc. (Philippians 4:18). Of course, that must have included "highly" things about them. This makes it clear that the Bible isn't asking us not to think highly of ourselves at all, but to refuse to think more highly than we are meant to. Instead, we are meant to think "soberly." The epistle to the Philippians gives us a clue into how this works.

Let nothing be done through selfish ambition or conceit, but in lowliness of mind, let each esteem others better than himself. Let each of you look out not only for his own interests, but also for the interests of others. Let this mind be in you which was also in Christ Jesus who, being in the form of God, thought it not robbery to be equal with God, but made Himself of no reputation, taking the form of a bondservant... (Philippians 2:3-7)

The phrases, "lowliness of mind" and "esteem others better than himself," are quite sufficient clues to help us understand what it means to think soberly. Then, the expression, "let each look out not only for his interests but also for... others" sums it all up. In today's terms, this means that whatsoever we desire or want shouldn't be more important than the needs of others. By thinking lowly of ourselves, and esteeming others better than we are, we are more concerned about serving. Now, this doesn't mean we'll abandon our dreams and personal ambitions; what it means is that we will be less selfish with them.

Keeping our ambitions in perfect sync with our ministry and service to others is fundamental. This means we should be pleased with whatever capacity that allows us do this effectively. This may mean our responsibilities in our family, community, church, and etc. Trying to outgrow platforms that avail us the privilege to serve God through exhorting others, meeting their needs, prayers and intercessions, etc. may mean we are getting too ambitious to follow God's will. Of course, there is an exception if we are genuinely seeking platforms that allow us to do these things in bigger ways.

I once read about a wealthy CEO of a very successful multinational, who served as a Bible study class teacher in his small church of barely one hundred adults. As one of the three Bible study teachers in the church, he was surely not occupying the most esteemed position in the church. Now, as a Bible study teacher, he followed the instructions of the pastor, who was just a younger man of much lower financial abilities. Under different circumstances, the pastor, as a regular person, would have found it extremely difficult even to secure an appointment to meet with him. They were certainly far apart, going by their financial and social statuses. Yet, the wealthy CEO understood that it was his ministry to serve as a Bible study teacher under the supervision of this pastor. He didn't see himself as a wealthy CEO of a multinational firm in the church. Rather, he saw himself as one who was there to do God's will by serving men. I think he is an apt example of someone with "lowliness of mind," who "esteems others better than himself." Indeed, he is a clear example of one who isn't just about his own interests, but also the interests of others.

Like I said earlier, I have had moments when I was faced with temptations to compromise on serving God for personal ambitions. There were times I actually compromised. But, thank God, I didn't always take too long to get back on track. Thus, I understand that several Christian women all around the world are constantly faced with such experiences. Sometimes, what you experience is the feeling that you can do more for yourself by either neglecting your family, or other people God has brought to you. Other times, it is giving up on jobs that allow you enough time for fellowship with God and his people for other jobs that spare you no time for these, all for some personal gains. It may even be the feeling that you aren't getting the praise or the honor you deserve from serving God's people.

Women who sacrifice their time, potential working hours, etc. to create time to take care of their family and properly raise their kids, may sometimes feel they are losing out on some sort of benefit out there. However, the fact is that carrying out your responsibilities at home is also a fundamental part of your service to God. In Chapter 5, I cited an example of Susana Wesley, a woman who made it her ministry to intercede for family and raise children who would change the world. She eventually succeeded at it. However, she and her family were battled with much challenges all through these times.

There are several circumstances in which you may find yourself, which may create a desire to abandon God's will. One thing you have to understand is the fact that God is aware of what you are going through. *For we do not have a high priest who cannot sympathize with our weaknesses, but was in all points tempted as we are, yet without sin (Hebrews 4:15).* It is important that you bear in mind that God understands that you are genuinely being tempted. He isn't waiting for you to fail so that He will pounce on you.

Since God cares about us carrying out His will and doing the things that we are supposed to do, He is willing to help us during difficult times. Apostle Paul succinctly captures this fact in his words, *no temptation has overtaken you except such as is common to man; but God is faithful, who will not allow you to be tempted beyond what you are able (1 Corinthians 10:13).* In other words, God has equipped us with the abilities to overcome whatever temptations we are faced with. No temptation, beyond our abilities, can come near us. Hence, it becomes important to trust Him to guide us through such tempting times and to help us align ourselves with His will. David expresses this fact in one of his popular psalms, *the Lord is my shepherd; I shall not want… He leads me in the paths of righteousness for His name's sake (Psalm 23: 1, 3).* Besides, we also have examples from the Scriptures to learn from. The story of Miriam is one that can be of huge blessings to every woman.

Miriam: A Jealous Prophetess

Miriam was a prophetess and a sister to Moses and Aaron. She suddenly surfaced in the book of Exodus, after God rescued the Israelites from the hands of Pharaoh and his soldiers. From her activities, it isn't hard to tell that she was a leader in Israel, particularly amongst Israel. The Egyptian chariots and horsemen and all the host of Pharaoh were swallowed by the sea, from which the Israelites were delivered, the Bible records:

Then Miriam the prophetess, the sister of Aaron, took the tumbrel in her hand, and all the women went out after her with tumbrels and with dances. And Miriam answered them: "sing unto the Lord, for He has triumphed gloriously! The horse and its rider, He has thrown into the sea" (Exodus 15:20-21).

After this point, the next time we read of Miriam in the Bible is when she and Aaron speak against Moses.

Then Miriam and Aaron spoke against Moses because of the Ethiopian woman whom they had married; for he had married an Ethiopian woman. So they said, "Has the Lord indeed spoken through Moses? Has He not spoken through me also?" And the Lord heard it (Numbers 12:1-2).

Here, even though they seemed to be making a case out of Moses' choice of wife, the statements that followed showed otherwise. It appears that they were expressing their jealousy under the pretext of blaming him for marrying the wrong woman. This is quite obvious from their statements. Now, Bible scholars have argued that Miriam was the primary speaker and instigator here. The fact that her name was mentioned first proves this. Also, the fact that she was the only one who eventually got punished gives us another reason to go with this theory. Besides, since she is the example we are examining, we will be dwelling more on her.

Being a prophetess and also a leader in Israel, Miriam must have thought, within her, that she wasn't getting all the praise she deserved. She must have seen Moses as a threat to her; hence, the expression, "the Lord doesn't speak through Moses only. Has He not spoken also by us?" She probably wanted more leadership privileges and respect in Israel, just like Moses. We have every reason to believe that Miriam didn't just begin to allow such thoughts that day. This must have been the gurgitation of her mind for a long time. Jesus lets us know this in His words, *out of the abundance of the heart, the mouth speaks (Matthew 12:34)*. In response to Miriam and Aaron's thoughts against Moses, God showed up and called them to Himself, saying:

Hear now my words: If there is a prophet among you, I, the Lord, make myself known unto Him in a vision; I speak to him in a dream. Not so with my servant Moses: he is faithful in all my house. I speak with him face to face, even plainly and not in dark sayings; and he sees the form of the Lord. Why then were you not afraid to speak against my servant Moses (Exodus 12:6-8)?

From the Lord's sayings, we can see that the thoughts of Miriam and Aaron were directly addressed. They had definitely thought more highly of themselves than they ought to have thought. They exalted themselves in their minds to be contemporaries of Moses. Against Miriam's picture of herself as a prophetess and leader who in the rank of Moses, the Lord spoke differently. He communicated plainly and "face to face" with Moses, and not in dark sayings, through dreams and visions as he did with other prophets. The Bible records that the anger of the Lord was aroused against them, and Miriam became leprous (Numbers 12:9).

It is unlikely that God was angry with Miriam and Aaron just because they spoke against Moses. That wasn't the first time anyone would speak against him. Pharaoh, Zipporah, his wife, and the children of Israel had spoken against Moses in the past without being punished for it. God rebuked Miriam and Moses just to correct their envy, jealously, and most importantly, their selfish ambition.

As we earlier saw, Miriam was a prophetess and was, to an extent, a leader in Israel, especially among women. Now, if only she had decided to solely pay her attention to doing what God had chosen her to do, she would have found it easier to overcome her ungodly ambitiousness. If she had learned to do nothing through selfish ambition, have lowliness of mind, esteem others better than herself, and look out for the interests of others instead of hers (Philippians 2:3-4), she would definitely not have gotten into trouble.

Avoiding Miriam's Jealousy

As emotional beings, we are always likely to feel hurt when we think we aren't getting the attention, praise, or the benefits we deserve. It is absolutely normal to feel this way. In fact, it is just right to express our grievances sometimes. At your workplace, for instance, you definitely wouldn't be out of order to communicate your concerns to the appropriate persons or department. Similarly, there isn't anything wrong with fighting for one's civil and political rights. However, in doing God's will, our desires and rights come only secondarily to doing the will of God.

Our service to God means we choose to sacrifice our own desires, pleasure and wants. We find this example with our Lord, Jesus Christ and His apostles. Apostle Paul, a man who wrote about half of the New Testament books, constantly bears witness to this: *Now if we are afflicted, it is for your consolation and salvation, which is effective for enduring the same sufferings which we suffer (2 Corinthians 1:6). But in all things, we commend ourselves as ministers of God: in much patience, in tribulations... (2 Corinthians 6:4).*

Thoughts of selfishness and pride often tend to creep into our minds, thus, weakening one's desire to be an intercessor, serve other believers, or be involved in any means of service to God. Sometimes, such thoughts may spring from some ill-treatment or embarrassment you have encountered in the course of such service. I understand that such times may be difficult; I have had several such experiences. However, the fact remains that you are doing all you are doing for God, and not for the people who discourage you. The sufferings we have encountered shouldn't turn our backs against doing what God's desires for us. Under the influence of the Holy Spirit, Paul admonished Timothy, *but you be watchful in all things, endure afflictions… fulfill your ministry (2 Timothy 4:5).*

Thinking about Miriam, I can imagine she must have had a reason or two for comparing herself to Moses. First, she was Moses' elder sister and probably watched him grow up. She must have also been actively involved in the exodus of the Israelites from Egypt. In the process of this, she must have put in so much work and probably been through many sufferings. However, her error was allowing all her emotions and ambition supersede her sense of service to God.

Sometimes, we may actually have a few seemingly good reasons to get selfishly ambitious. We may allow thoughts of what we deserve to come to our minds. Thinking from the natural perspective, you may feel you deserve just whatever you desire. And you may even begin to consider some compromising means of compensating yourself, which may include neglecting your family, the people God has sent you to or the things He has asked you to do. When thoughts or suggestions like this come to my mind, I often respond by thinking on two verses of Scripture. The first is taken from the book of Peter: *Therefore humble yourselves under the mighty hand of God, that He may exalt you in due time (1 Peter 5:6).* The second is taken from the book of Hebrews: *For God is not unjust to forget your work and labor of love which you have shown towards His name, in that you have ministered to the saints and do minister (Hebrews 6:10).* These verses bring my attention to the fact that it is only God who can exalt and reward me for my efforts. I can't sufficiently reward myself.

Let This Mind Be in You

Let this mind be in you which was also in Christ Jesus who, being in the form of God, thought it not robbery to be equal with God, but made Himself of no reputation, taking the form of a bondservant, and coming in the likeness of sinful men… He humbled Himself and became obedient to the point of death, even the death of the cross. Therefore God also has highly exalted Him and given Him the name which is above every name (Philippians 2:5-9)

Here, Paul admonishes the church to pattern their thinking after Christ's humility. His presentation of the example of Christ is a stupendously rich analogy to give us a picture of what we must be like in our walk in God's will. Paul lets us see that even though our Lord Jesus had every reason to make Himself equal with God on earth, He chose to present Himself completely as a man, allowing Himself to be insulted, beaten, and eventually killed in the hands of ordinary men.

John describes Jesus Christ as the incarnation of the word of God which had been from the beginning, and which is also God Himself: *In the beginning was the Word, and the Word was with God, and the Word was God… And the Word became flesh and dwelt among us (John 1:1, 14).* Jesus Himself often expressed this in His words: *…I am from above. You are of this world; I am not of this world (John 8:23). …He who has seen Me has seen the Father… (John 14:9). I and My Father are one ((John 10:30).* The epistle to Timothy even helps us see this in a clearer light, in how it describes the incarnation of Christ: *God was manifest in the flesh, justified in the Spirit, seen by angels, preached among the Gentiles, believed on in the world, received up into glory (1 Timothy 3:16).*

As Christians, we understand that Jesus was the incarnation of God in human flesh. Apparently, this is why Paul made a big case of Jesus' life on earth as a perfect example of humility for us to follow. Paul expresses the fact that Jesus was in the **form** of God. Now, Greek scholars let us know that the word, "form," as used here, comes from the Greek word, "*morphe*," which means a nature or an appearance. This means that Jesus, even though He was a deity, took upon the complete nature of a normal human being. He had feelings and felt pains like humans do. We have records in the gospel accounts (Matthew, Mark, Luke and John) that bears witness to the fact that he felt hungry, tired, and physical pains just like every other human. The book of Hebrews also shows us that He also suffered temptations like men do (Hebrews 6:10). He took this nature upon Himself, even though He was Divinity in human flesh.

Another striking point to also note in Paul's analogy is the fact that *Jesus Christ humbled Himself, and became obedient to the point of death…(Philippians 2:8).* He didn't just stop at just becoming a man, He totally left behind His great power and authority and subjected Himself to be flogged, slapped, stripped, spat on, mocked, and eventually killed by mere men. Now, this was all in a bid to save all humans, including even those who spat on Him. He was all out to fulfill the will of the father. The truth is that He could have chosen to act otherwise. He had the power and authority to demonstrate for all to see.

The night in which Jesus was taken, Peter attacked one of those sent to arrest Him and cut off his ears. But, Jesus' response showed that He was truly subjecting Himself to be taken and killed. The gospel account of Luke records that Jesus healed and restored the servant's ear (Luke 22: 51). The gospel account of Matthew adds an extra interesting detail; Jesus said to Peter, *put your sword in its place… or do you think I cannot now pray to My Father, and He will provide Me with more than twelve legions of angels (Matthew 26:52-53)?* Jesus had admitted earlier that He was the one willfully laying down His life and that no one was taking it from Him, that He had the power to lay it down and the power to take it again (John 10:18).

Finally, Paul lets us see the end result of Jesus' total submission: *therefore God also has highly exalted Him and given Him the name which is above every name (Philippians 2:9).* Well, God exalting Jesus Christ here wouldn't be in the sense at which you reward another person. It speaks about the authority that is in the name of Jesus. In other words, God, the Father, chooses to be reached in none else but only in the name of Jesus Christ; God chooses to be identified only in Jesus Christ: *for in Him dwells all the fullness of the Godhead bodily (Colossians 2:9).* When we meditate further on this, we come to the conclusion that God associates Himself only with acts of humility; He is found in nothing else but in this. This is simply why Jesus had said to His disciples:

...but whoever desires to become great among you shall be your servant. And whosoever of you desires to be the first shall be the slave of all. For even the Son of Man did not come to be served but to give His life as a ransom for many (Matthew 10:43-45).

In following the examples of Jesus Christ, we become less likely to be selfish or overambitious. Jesus submitted Himself to the hands of man completely, even though He had all the power to choose otherwise. He was sold out to the cause of laying down His life for the sins of men. Now, Paul says, "let this mind be in you." In other words, we are required to cultivate the same pattern of thinking that Jesus had. This means that we shouldn't be all out to seek what glorifies us, but God only. While going about our daily life and activities, we should choose to serve and not to be served. It is in submitting ourselves to serve God and men, laying down our praises, honors, achievements, etc. that we get true honor and exaltation.

Chasing after Faithfulness not Success

We all naturally like to be successful in all we do. This is why we work so hard in our jobs and businesses. We often think of expansion: expanding our businesses, finances, influence, knowledge, abilities, and etc. This is natural to every human. However, when we constantly chase after success without considering the need to be faithful, we become vulnerable to greed and all sorts of evil thinking. In fact, one of the most common signs that someone is overambitious is that they suddenly disregard the need to be faithful. This is often found in the business world. When an organization gets suddenly overambitious, they may resort to all sorts of shenanigans to manipulate customers or to attract deals.

As Christian women, it is important to pay less emphasis on our own constant desires and to ensure that we maintain a culture of faithfulness. By this, I am not playing down or discouraging the need to aim to be successful. But, whatever success we are aiming for should be one that doesn't cause us to be self-centered. Every success that we aim for in life should be one that allows us to be faithful before God and men. This is possible only when we live our lives with the consciousness of doing God's will. We need to bear in mind that we are accountable to God.

Faithfulness is surely one of the most important qualities that we require, as humans, before entrusting anyone with any responsibility that is important to us. This is found in the business world, corporate world, politics, and even in informal social settings. We are naturally attracted to faithful people. This is the same thing before God. Being a faithful God, He desires that we are also faithful to Him. God desires that we are not obsessed about achieving our own personal successes. It is with this understanding that the epistle to Timothy instructs (reading from the International Standard Version), *what you have heard from me through many witnesses, entrust to faithful people who will be able to teach others as well (2 Timothy 2:2).*

God wouldn't trust anyone with His responsibilities, except they are faithful. In the first epistle to Timothy, the apostle Paul admitted that his appointment into ministry was possible only because God counted him faithful (1 Timothy 1:12). Among the requirements for one's qualification to be an overseer, the same epistle reads, *likewise, their wives must be reverent… faithful in all things (1 Timothy 3:11).* We desire only faithful people to work with us; God desires this even more. He requires that we are faithful in all things.

We walk in faithfulness when we show our accountability in the responsibilities that He has committed us. We are accountable to God for our family, for the people He has linked us with for the purpose of service, and for the simple tasks that He has put in our hearts to do for Him. We show our faithfulness in how we raise our kids, how we show kindness to our neighbors, how we inspire others, how we preach God's words to others, how we show good examples to our colleagues at work, etc. It is our responsibility to keep ourselves constantly in pursuit of faithfulness in these things, instead of being blinded by the pursuit of worldly success.

Prayer

Dear Father, thank You for teaching me to be selfless in my service to You and all the men and women around me. Thank You for Your word which guides me and to puts me constantly in check when I err. I choose to have the mind of Christ and to submit myself constantly to Your will. I choose to be faithful in all I do in Jesus' name. Amen!

A Glance through Your Bible
Philippians 2:3-9; Romans 12:3-5

Philippians 2:3 Let nothing be done through selfish ambition or conceit, but in lowliness of mind, let each esteem others better than himself. ⁴Let each of you look not out only for his own interests, but also for the interests of others. ⁵Let this mind be in you which was also in Christ Jesus, ⁶who, being in the form of God, did not consider it robbery to be equal with

God, ⁷but made Himself of no reputation, taking the form of a bondservant, and coming in the likeness of sinful men. ⁸And being found in appearance as a man, He humbled Himself and became obedient to the point of death, even the death of the cross. ⁹Therefore, God also has highly exalted Him and given Him the name which is above every name…

Romans 12:3 For I say, through the grace given to me, to everyone who is among you, not to think of himself more highly than he ought to think, but to think soberly, as God has dealt to each one a measure of faith. ⁴For as we have many members in one body, but all the members do not have the same function, ⁵so we, being many, are one body in Christ, and individually members of one another.

Study Questions

- What is the connection between our thinking and the tendency to get ambitious?
- How exactly should we think to keep ourselves in check against selfish ambitions?
- Why were Miriam and Aaron rebuked by God?
- What example of humility do we find in Jesus' actions?
- How can we follow the examples of Jesus' in our daily life?
- How can we strike the right balance between our success and faithfulness to God?

9

You May Be Misunderstood

"Why should they be against me when I am only trying to help them?" These were the words Liz uttered to me almost absentmindedly, as she sank into a chair at my office many years ago. Besides being a lecturer and an older colleague to me, Liz was a women's rights activist that I really admired. She devoted much of her time and resources holding conferences and traveling to visit rural communities, for the purpose of educating women and girls on their rights in the society. She was, and still is, a part of several NGOs, some of which she founded or co-founded, for the purpose of pursuing the single cause of emancipating women and girls from their unfair limitations in the society. However, she had come under severe criticism, most of which came from some of the women who were benefiting from her activities. She lamented this bitterly before me, as she sat at my office that afternoon.

Listening to Liz, I could tell she really meant well for the women and girls she was fighting for. But, for some unclear reasons, some of these women spoke publicly against her and incited others to do the same. While she received hundreds of positive messages on her email and social media platforms appreciating her for her efforts, she also encountered some toxic messages which broke her heart. Having devoted her time, energies and her resources to the cause, she didn't expect any woman to speak to her or about her so hatefully.

I could tell very clearly that Liz was just being misunderstood by the women who spoke against her. When I expressed this to her, "but what is there to misunderstand about our sheer protest of goodwill," she retorted. "Well," I said, "nobody has ever been understood by everyone, in the history of humankind." Now, this is absolutely true! Some of the most revered personalities in our global history were hated by a handful of those who lived in their days. Even though they are revered by many people today, many still do not agree with what they stood for.

Irrespective of the good we are doing, there will always be those who have negative opinions about us. These are the people who misunderstand us. Now, even though we may be upset about this, we have to know that this is just normal; it is a reality that we have to learn to live with. I have learned, over the years, never to expect everyone to understand me, irrespective of the good things I do, or how excellently I do them. When you expect only praises and love from everyone, you'd probably soon be heading for a disappointment. You will certainly be misunderstood.

Now, we cannot deny that one of the toughest realities we are likely to face in our resolution to serve God and humanity is to have our intentions misunderstood. Irrespective of the little fraction of those who misunderstand us compared to those who support us, we are likely to still feel somewhat concerned. This is even made worse at times when our families, friends, or closest allies are among those who speak against the things we do. Feelings of discouragement, apathy and even depression may set in at times like these, causing us to want to give up on the things we do. However, we always have a choice to decide how we respond.

The Scripture lets us see that we can choose how we respond to such trying times like these. The epistle of James says, *my brethren, count it all joy when you fall into various trials, knowing that the testing of your faith produces patience (James 1:2-3)*. We find a similar admonition in the epistle to the Romans: *...we also glory in tribulations, knowing that tribulation produces perseverance; and perseverance, character; and character, hope (Romans 5:3-4)*. Thus, we see that we can choose to rejoice during these times. When we choose not to be deterred by the fact that many are against us, we are expressing our faith in God and in His words. We know that, by enduring such difficult times and choosing to be joyful in them, we are developing character. This means the criticisms we face from those who aim to discourage us would only end up adding to us and make us stronger if we choose to respond to them rightly. Such times are really meant to strengthen our convictions.

Why You May Be Misunderstood

When we encounter people who criticize us for doing the good things we do, we may be tempted to assume that they are just some lousy and unpleasant people who just hate us for no reason. Well, this is likely not to be the case most of the time. The most probable reason why anyone would speak against you for doing something good without any selfish ambition is that they misunderstand you. Their reason for criticizing you may be due to their misunderstanding of your idea, original intentions, or your personality. Now, this isn't necessarily their fault. Often times, it is due to their past experiences or fears. People who have had several negative experiences, for instance, may be paranoid and would get suspicious when they encounter persons who are genuinely willing to help. Similarly, friends, allies, or family members may just be afraid that you are on the wrong track. Thus, they break ties with you, hoping not to be a part of your failures.

It is important for us not to get vindictive against those who misunderstand us. The fact is that we may be doing the same thing if we were in their shoes. Sometimes, I think about the story of Mary, the mother of Jesus; how she became pregnant supernaturally, without any physical means. The Bible describes that *she was found with child of the Holy Spirit*

(Matthew 1:18). Now, this was after an angel appeared to her and told her she would conceive and give birth to Jesus (Luke 1:31). However, I think about the problems she must have had trying to convince others that the pregnancy was supernatural. Even Joseph, to whom she was betrothed, needed a supernatural encounter with an angel too before believing her. He had determined to put her away (Matthew 1: 19-23).

Now, I surely do not blame everyone who must doubted Mary. I probably would have done the same too. Like Joseph, I would have required the supernatural appearance of an angel to believe Mary's story which, by the way, must have sounded like a "fairy tale" to even her closest family members and allies. Thinking about how implausible Mary's story must have sounded to those who heard her helps me relate with the fact that many cannot just help it but misunderstand things they cannot relate with. Some probably wouldn't believe that you have no selfish intention for your services, since they cannot fathom any human being do something so selfless. It is beyond their scope of reasoning. Friends and allies may think you are losing your mind for being passionate about a course that really doesn't benefit you in any way. They may not understand you are simply after the will of God. Others may think you are against them in some way by doing what you are doing. The point is that they are all failing to understand you.

It is natural for others to misunderstand us irrespective of whether or not we are of benefit to them with what we do. This is even more intense when we choose to stay with the will of God. Doing the will of God surely doesn't make sense to people who aren't spiritually-focused. The Bible lets us know that *the natural man doesn't receive the things of the spirit of God, for they are foolishness to him (1 Corinthians 2:14).* Hence, as women who are passionate about ensuring that the will of God prevails, we will surely be understood by people who aren't as passionate. They may see us as either foolish or with some ulterior motive when we constantly walk in the will of God. Some others may see us as overambitious. This may even make them hate us. Jesus lets us know this in His word: *If you were of the world, the world would love its own. Yet, because you are not of the world, but I chose you out of the world, therefore the world hates you (John 15:19).*

Dealing with Misunderstanding the Jesus Way

Our Lord Jesus is the ideal picture of one who was totally misunderstood. Despite His good works, healing the sick, feeding multitudes, raising the dead, etc., He was highly crucified by even those who benefited from His miraculous works. Eventually, He was arrested and crucified with the approval of some of the people whom He once healed, fed, whose relatives He had once raised from the dead, cleansed of leprosy etc. Jesus didn't respond with vindictively. He knew that they were not really being themselves; He knew that they surely misunderstood Him somehow. As He bled to death on the cross, Jesus only chose to pray for them, *Father, forgive them, for they do not know what they do (Luke 23:34).*

The fact that they misunderstood Him and treated Him badly, despite all the good He had done didn't cause Him to give up His assignment of caring for them and saving them. Jesus did this to show us an example to follow. Thus, it is incumbent on us to remain firm in doing the will of God, irrespective of the criticisms of others. We have to keep loving all persons (including those who misunderstand us); we have to keep serving them, praying for them, and choosing not to get bitter against them, irrespective of how much wrong they have done to us.

As Christians, we have to understand that we can have the same kind of mindset that Jesus has. His way of thinking and acting should be native to us, as a people who have His spirit residing in us. Hence, we can actually think the way He does and, as a result, act the way He acts. The epistle to the Philippians helps us see that this is possible, *Let this mind be in you which also was in Christ (Philippians 2:5).* Jesus' life on earth leaves us an example of how we should act. Interestingly, we can actually do these things too, because His spirit in us strengthens us to do the same. We should be able to say, like Paul, *I can do all things through Christ who strengthens me (Philippians 4:13).*

Having sacrificed your convenience, resources, time, energies, etc. to do God's will by selflessly reaching out to meeting human needs, all you desire is some form of encouragement. You only crave some sort of moral support to keep you doing the same and to do even more. At such times, you are emotionally vulnerable. This is particularly peculiar to women since we are generally more emotional. And, the beautiful thing is, once we get the encouragement we desire, we can get stirred up from within, refreshed, and able to much more. However, on the other hand, we can be vulnerable to feelings of discouragement, when other people criticize us unfairly or speak ill of the good things we are doing. This is likely to culminate in feelings of bitterness, which makes us want to quit the good we are doing. Here is where we have to understand that Jesus is our example and the clear picture of the things that we can and should do.

Not once did Jesus decide to hate anyone or quit the good that He was known to do, just because someone spoke ill of Him; He was known to be after the good of all persons He ever encountered. He Himself was the perfect example of what He preached, *love your enemies, bless them that curse you, do good to those who hate you, and pray for those who spitefully use you and persecute you (Matthew 5:44)*. He constantly walked in love to those who hated Him. Once, when He visited Nazareth, a city in which He had grown up, and taught in their synagogue, the people wondered where He got His knowledge from. Thus, they were offended and spoke ill of Him. Yet, the Bible records that *He laid His hands on a few sick people and healed them (Mark 6:5)*. He expressed His love to them by healing them, despite the fact that they despised Him. He didn't stop there, He marveled at their unbelief in His abilities, their misunderstanding of His personality, and went around the whole city teaching them (Mark 6:6).

Jesus' example at Nazareth gives us the perfect blueprint for how we can respond to similar situations. When criticized, we can choose to be unfazed, maintaining our stay in the will of God. We can choose to keep doing good things that even our detractors can benefit from. This isn't a sign of weakness, but a clear demonstration of the strength we find in Jesus Christ. Also, we can be patient with people who do not understand us. Instead of abandoning the people of Nazareth for literally rejecting Him, Jesus went about the whole city teaching the people. This means we can also be patient with people who misunderstand us, helping them see our true intentions.

The Ability to Stay on Track

Staying on track and following the examples of Jesus surely can't be by our human abilities. It is certainly impossible to stay with the will of God through persecutions and criticisms solely by our human abilities. The Scriptures help us see this: ...*for by strength, no man shall prevail (1 Samuel 2:9); Not by power nor by might, but by My spirit, says the Lord of hosts (Zechariah 4:6).* The reason why Jesus could do the things He did on earth as a man had to be by His dependence on something that isn't human. Peter describes this in the book of Acts: *how God anointed Jesus Christ with the Holy Spirit and with power who went about doing good… (Acts 10:38)*. We find out that the Holy Spirit is the reason for His supernatural love walk. The beautiful thing is that we have the same Holy Spirit given to us, as believers in the gospel of Jesus Christ. Paul lets us see this in the letter to the Ephesians: *In Him [Christ] you also trusted, after that you heard the word of truth, the gospel of your salvation; in whom also, having believed, you were sealed with the Holy Spirit of promise (Ephesians 1:13)*.

Now, with the Holy Spirit inside of us, we have the ability to act just the same ways Jesus did. This means we have the capacity to be loving to those who persecute and despise us, we have the ability to be patient, and to stay on track with the will of God. Paul, in the book of Romans, helps us learn this reality: *…because the love of God has been poured out in our hearts by the Holy Spirit who is given to us (Romans 5:5)*. This means we have the spiritual capacity to love others deep in our spirits. Just like Jesus, we do not have to struggle to love those who hate us, bless and do only good to them, even when they persecute us. The same capacity that made Jesus do these things is resident in us too.

Several years ago, when I first encountered the Scriptures that spoke about the Holy Spirit being in every believer of the gospel of Jesus Christ, I was excited. Nevertheless, I was doubtful for a few reasons. First, being a believer, I wondered why I found it difficult to do things that should naturally come from someone who has the Holy Spirit. I had been brought up to believe that everyone with the Holy Spirit is supposed to be just perfect and with no fault. Well, I was wrong. Through the years, I have come to understand better. Having the Holy Spirit in you doesn't necessarily translate to an automatic perfection. There is a part for us to play as recipients of the spirit of God. This part is to walk in the Spirit. *Walk in the Spirit, and you shall not fulfill the lust of the flesh (Galatians 5:16).* This lets us see that there are tendencies of taking the wrong steps, even though one has the Holy Spirit. Hence, the need to walk in the Spirit.

Now, in walking in the Spirit, we understand that there are specific traits that should come from the Spirit. Of course, these are the traits we find in Jesus Christ. This means, when we take deliberate steps to walk like He did, we would be walking in the Spirit. More plainly, Paul lets us see these traits thus:

But the fruit of the Spirit is love, joy, peace, longsuffering, kindness, goodness, faithfulness, gentleness, self-control… And those who are Christ's have crucified the flesh with its passions and desires. If we live in the Spirit, let us also walk in the Spirit (Galatians 5:22-25)

Since we are Christ's, our reality is that we have crucified the flesh and its lusts; we now live in the Spirit. What this means is that we have received the spiritual enablement to live beyond our natural selfish cravings. It means we can actually walk in the spirit of God just like Jesus did if we choose to. We can live our lives in service to God and all persons, irrespective of the challenges we encounter and the criticisms we face. We can choose not to be weighed down by those who misunderstand us but to respond to them with love. *As the Father has sent Me, I also send you (John 20:21)*, Jesus said to us, letting us know that we can do the will of God unwaveringly, as He did.

Drawing Joy from Within

When fiercely attacked, criticized, and persecuted by oppositions, there may be very little to be happy about. Looking around us, at such times, we have some reasons to be sad, angry, despondent, and doubtful of God's presence with us. However, there is something that we can draw out from the inside of us: it is called joy! We do not have to react based on our natural human impulses by being sad, we can actually draw joy from the inside of us. I call this "living from the inside out."

As children of God with the Holy Spirit inside of us, we have the capacity to be always joyful when we go through difficult times. This isn't due to any human quality or ability; rather, it is a result of the qualities that the Holy Spirit produces on the inside of us. This is why the apostles can write to the church: *count it all joy when you fall into various trials (James 1:2); Rejoice in the Lord always (Philippians 4:4); but rejoice to the extent that you partake of Christ's sufferings (1Peter 4:13).* They surely understood that joy isn't really based on the good experiences we have, but that it is a quality that we have on the inside of us. The same way we have the capacity to love, we can always be joyful too. It is a fruit of God's spirit in us: *But the fruit of the Spirit is love, **joy**, peace, longsuffering, kindness, goodness, faithfulness, gentleness, self-control... (Galatians 5:22-23).*

It is solely our choice to be joyful, just as it is to be loving. We can choose not to be bitter and angry when we are misunderstood and criticized unfairly. The capacity to be joyful is within us. James gives us an apt recipe to being joyful. He encourages us to be joyful, ***knowing that the testing of your faith produces patience** (James 1:3)*. The knowing that our difficult times have come to make us stronger and to make us more virtuous is what makes being joyful possible, even during difficult situations. This is exactly what Paul means too when he says, *knowing that tribulation produces perseverance (Romans 5:3)*. We simply have to know that we aren't losing out during these times. Rather, we are being equipped to be even better.

We find the apostles in the habit of rejoicing every time they went through some sort of opposition. Once, when they were beaten for preaching, *they departed..., rejoicing that they were counted worthy to suffer shame for His name (Acts 5:41)*. Paul expressed, *I now rejoice in my sufferings (Col 1:24)*. The history of the early church is filled with instances of church leaders expressing their joy in the serious persecutions, even to the points of their martyrdom. This just shows that joy is not a phenomenon that comes from our happy experiences. It is a state of heart that we can stir up within us anytime. Irrespective of the negative circumstances around us, we can always be joyful.

Building Conviction

A few years ago, I decided to see every trying time that comes my way as some sort of examination meant to prove the veracity or authenticity of my convictions. Since I believe so much in what I do and I am convinced that it is the will of God for me, no one's criticism should bring me down. This is why it is important to start out with enough clarity and to be sure that what you are doing is God's will for you. That way, you'd be drawing enough strength to face the opposition squarely and to stay joyful during trying times. One common reason why people give up on the things that they do when they go through trying times, is their lack of conviction. The book of Proverbs helps us see this: *If you faint in the day of adversity, your strength is small (Proverbs 24:10)*. When convinced that you are on the right track and that you are living in sync with the will of God, it is easier to stay firm, joyful, and unshaken through hard times. Your conviction helps you see that you are on the ideal course for your life. Even if the whole world is against you, you can always tell that God is with you.

The apostles of Jesus and the early church fathers could face all kinds of severe persecutions and lay down their lives because they were convinced about their cause. Their conviction was the door to the joy and strength with which they faced severe torments and hardships. It would have been impossible to pull through the trials they faced, without being totally convinced. Similarly, we wouldn't stand a chance, without being fully convinced that we are living out the plan of God for our lives by doing the things we do.

Now, conviction doesn't come to us randomly, or by accident. It is built and cultivated in moments of fellowship with God. Serious actions and decisions that are personal to us require that we examine their authenticity through prayers, God's word, and some moment of self-reflection before we can reach the level of conviction to keep us going through tempting times. I have divided the practical ways (or steps) to building conviction into three: Fellowship with God through prayers, Fellowship with God through His word, and Self-reflection.

Fellowship with God through Prayers

A prayerful life is surely one of the most indispensable factors to fulfilling the will of God for our lives. This is clearly proven in the multiple verses of Scriptures that instruct us on the need to pray always. Jesus, our Lord, tells us unequivocally, *men ought always to pray and not to lose heart (Luke 18:1)*. The epistles are also filled with several other similar instructions, instructing Christians to pray always: *praying always with all prayers and supplications... (Ephesians 6:18), continue earnest in prayer (Colossians 4:2), pray without ceasing (1 Thessalonians 5:17), I desire that men pray everywhere (1 Timothy 2:8), be watchful in your prayers (1 Peter 4:7).*

Jesus leaves us a comprehensive example of how we can constantly live in the Spirit and fulfill His will for our lives. He was a man of prayer! The records of Matthew, Mark, Luke and John show us how He was constantly found praying. Studying His life through just the gospel of Luke, it is easy to see that Jesus lived a life that placed premium on the constancy of prayer. Here are a few instances:

*When all the people were baptized, it came to pass that Jesus also was baptized, **and while He prayed**... (Luke 3:21).*

*...great multitudes came together to hear, and to be healed by Him of their infirmities. So **He Himself withdrew into the wilderness and prayed** (Luke 5:15-16).*

*Now, it came to pass in those days that **He went out to the mountain to pray**, and continued all night in prayer to God (Luke 6:12).*

*And it happened, **as He was alone praying**... Now it came to pass... that He took Peter, John, and James and **went up on the mountain to pray** (Luke 9: 18, 28)*

*Now it came to pass, as **He was praying in a certain place**... (Luke 11:1).*

For Jesus to have devoted so much time to prayers, it is

clear that prayer is a very fundamental ingredient in helping us stay in the will of God. It brings the reality of God's will to our thinking and helps us build greater conviction to do His will. Once, when Jesus was about to undergo His final mission of suffering and dying on the cross, the Bible records that He went to the place of prayer. While He prayed, the Bible records that *an angel appeared to Him from heaven, strengthening Him (Luke 22:42).* This shows us what happens to us when we pray, our convictions become deeper, and we are strengthened to do God's will.

Fellowship with God through His Word

I already explained in Chapter 4 that God's word is the surest place to learn His will. When we give ourselves to fellowshipping with God through His word, His will is rekindled in us, thus, deepening our convictions. A clear understanding of God's word, which comes through constant study, gives us enough clue to know whether or not we are walking in the will of God. The psalmist understood just this fact when he declared: *Your word is a lamp and a light unto my path (Psalm 119:105).*

It is important to note that God's word supersedes our feelings and human emotions. Hence, it should be the ideal source of inspiration for the important actions we take. This means shelving anything that isn't in agreement with God's word and staying true to the things He approves. When you are sure that you're doing what God's word says you should, and, having prayed about it, you feel the nudge to go ahead within you, then, you can be confident you are on the right track.

Self-reflection

Self-reflection means looking inwards and examining yourself. In the conventional sense of the term, it is meant to help build self-awareness, understand one's strengths and weaknesses, and to help one identify the things that matter most to them. However, in the context of this book and chapter, it is meant to help you identify whether or not you are really passionate about serving God. In other words, self-reflection helps you know if you have no hidden selfish desire for doing the things you do.

Taking some moment to self-reflect is a fundamental way of building conviction. This involves asking yourself some vital personal questions to help you ascertain what your desires really are. You can reflect on what you gain from doing the things you do if you'd still be as passionate without these. You can ask yourself if you are willing to quit if you find out what you are doing isn't God's will for you. Depending on your circumstances, there are several questions you can reflect on to help you discover if what you are really after is God's will.

When you get to a point of certainty about God's will, you are very less likely to be weighed down by other's misunderstanding of what you do. The strength to do what you do consistently, without wavering, comes from a firm sense that you are involved in a cause for which you can lay down your life. By constantly deepening our conviction, we will be better equipped and prepared to deal with misunderstandings and oppositions with love and joy.

Prayer

Dear Father, I remain passionate to serve You and to do only Your will irrespective of the persecutions and challenges that come my way. I choose to love and be patient with those who misunderstand me. I choose to be joyful always. I ask that I am constantly strengthened to walk in the way You lead me in every moment of my life. Amen.

A Glance through Your Bible

John 15:18-21; James 1:2-4

John 15:18 If the world hates you, you know that it hated Me before it hated you. 19If you were of the world, the world would love its own. Yet, because you are not of the world, but I chose you out of the world, therefore the world hates you. 20Remember the word that I said unto you. 'A servant is not greater than his master.' If they persecuted Me, they will also persecute you. If they kept My word, they will keep yours also. 21But all these things they will do to you for My name's sake, because they do not know Him who sent Me.

James 1:2 My brethren, count it all joy when you fall into various trials, ³knowing that the testing of your faith produces patience. ⁴But let patience have its perfect work, that you may be perfect and complete, lacking nothing.

Study Questions

- Why are you likely to be misunderstood?
- How should you respond to people who misunderstand you?
- As Christians, can we really follow the examples of Jesus?
- How can we draw joy from within?
- Why is conviction an important ingredient to keep us going through tough times?
- How can we build conviction?

10

Grace to Hold On

Keeping fit and staying in good shape are top priorities for me. This is why, every week, I make some time to engage in fitness exercises. Now, one form of exercise I really enjoy is jogging, not just for its effectiveness, but for the fact that it helps me build discipline and endurance. When I make up my mind to jog a specific distance, I find myself in a situation where I have to give it all it takes, until I reach the destination point. Unlike other forms of exercise, jogging helps me see and relate with the fact that there is a concrete and literal destination in view. This helps me endure the pain and weariness while still maintaining a good pace, as I approach my destination. However, one key quality that helps me do this is willpower, that inner drive to reach my goal. It is the strength that makes it easier to do the difficult.

Willpower doesn't only help us overcome physical difficulties and limitations, it also helps us thrive mentally and psychologically. Thus, it is the force that drives us towards the achievement of our targets at work, our goals for our bodies, relationships, learning, and etc. However, despite its indispensability to our success in several facets of our lives, willpower is insufficient in helping us stay with the will of God. Our spiritual experiences surely require much more than just our willpower. The epistle to the Romans tells us: *it is not of him who wills, nor of him who runs, but of God who shows mercy (Romans 9:16).*

Staying firm and focused on doing the things that pertain to the will of God surely requires our commitment and some effort on our part. Yet, the grace of God is what determines how much successful we turn out to be in these things. What this means is that, while we are doing what we ought to do to the best of our abilities, we also have to be conscious of the grace of God. We have to understand that it is the grace of God, in the first place, that is responsible for whatever we can do. The apostle Paul surely understood this. In his epistle to the Corinthians, he said, *But by the grace of God, I am what I am, and His grace towards me was not in vain; but I labored more abundantly than they all, yet not I, but the grace of God which was with me (1 Corinthians 15:10).* This simply lets us see that our efforts are not really our efforts after all, but a function of the grace of God with us.

When we understand that the grace of God is what keeps us secured in doing His will and making impacts in our world, we will function under less pressure. This would keep us away from trusting in our own strengths and abilities—which can disappoint, but in the grace of God, which is ever-dependable and trustworthy. Trusting in the grace of God helps us through the times when we are most vulnerable when our natural abilities are mostly ineffective. The truth is that there will always be such times. Irrespective of how gifted or talented we are, we cannot do so much by our own natural abilities.

We would surely encounter difficult and tempting times that exhaust our human strengths and willpower. At such times, what keeps us going is the strength that comes from the grace of God. Hence, the extent to which we go, during such times, would depend on the extent to which we rest on God's grace. When we recognize the fact that we are weak and that our abilities are insufficient, we will find it easier to get the grace work for us. In this line of thought, Paul recounts his experience:

And lest I should be exalted above measure by the abundance of revelation that is given to me, a messenger of Satan to buffet me, lest I be exalted above measure. Concerning this thing I pleaded with the Lord three times that it might depart from me. And He said to me, "My grace is sufficient for you, for my strength is made perfect in weakness." Therefore, most gladly, I will rather boast in my infirmities, that the power of Christ may rest upon me. Therefore, I will take pleasure in infirmities, in reproaches, in needs, in persecutions, in distresses, for Christ's sake. For when I am weak, then I am made strong (2 Corinthians 12:7-10).

Bible scholars are divided as to what Paul's "thorn in the flesh" means, in the context of this passage. Some have argued that it was some kind of persecution or opposition against him; some others are of the opinion that it was some physical limitation. However, what is clear to us is that this "thorn in the flesh" isn't something he was happy about; it was definitely not something nice! We can see that the moment he learns about the sufficiency of God's grace for him, he decides to boast and take pleasure in his persecutions, distress, infirmities or whatever his "thorn in the flesh" was. He understood that God's grace was powerful enough to cover up for his weaknesses. This same mentality should underline our service in the will of God.

The Moses Example

The man, Moses, is surely one of the most prominent figures in the Bible. He played a key role in the deliverance of the children of Israel from Egypt and led them through the wilderness. He was also the mediator of the Old Testament. Besides these, the first five books of the Bible are credited to him. Moses was such a colossal figure whose inspired writings seemed to set the tone for the writings of the other prophets in the Old Testament part of the Bible. However, going by his natural abilities, it is quite amazing he was arguably the most unlikely person to have led the Israelites. First, he was reluctant to serve God. Besides, he was a poor speaker, with no obvious leadership skills.

Moses was born at a time when it was unlikely for any child to survive. Pharaoh, out of the fear that the children of Israel were expanding and growing larger than the Egyptians, had commanded that all male children be killed at birth. When Moses was eventually born, his mother hid him for a while till she couldn't keep him any longer. Then, she made a basket, in which she kept the child, and placed it along the side of the river. Later, when Pharaoh's daughter came to bathe at the river, she found the child and took him into custody. Interestingly, she unknowingly hired Moses' biological mother as to nurse him.

Moses grew up as an adopted son of the Egyptian princess but retained a consciousness of his origin. Thus, the Bible records that he often visited his Hebrew brethren and looked at them with a sense of compassion. One of such times, when he saw an Egyptian beating one of his Hebrew brethren, he killed the Egyptian covertly, believing that his actions were hidden. The next day, when he saw two Hebrew brethren fighting, he tried to separate them, but got shocked when one of them exclaimed: *who hath made you a judge over us? Do you intend to kill me as you killed the Egyptian (Exodus 2:14)?* At this point, Moses realized that his deed was not hidden. When Pharaoh eventually heard about it and sought to kill him, he escaped to Midian.

Moses lived with the Priest of Midian, who gave him his

daughter, Zipporah, as wife. He worked as a shepherd and tended his father-in-law's flock. One of such times, an angel of the Lord appeared to him in a flame of fire and told him that the cries of the people of Israel had come unto the Lord. Thus, the Lord was sending him (Moses) to Pharaoh to bring the people of Israel out of Egypt to the Promised Land. But Moses was reluctant; he had several excuses not to go. First, he told the Lord, *who am I that I should go to Pharaoh, and that I should bring the children of Israel out of Egypt (Exodus 3:11)?* But the Lord answered by assuring him of His presence. Moses responded again, *indeed when I come to the children of Israel and say to them, "the God of your fathers has sent me to you," they shall say unto me, "what is His name?" what shall I say to them (Exodus 3:13)?* But the Lord graciously answered him, *tell them I AM has sent you (Exodus 3:14).*

Again, Moses said, *But suppose they will not believe me or listen to my voice; suppose they say, "The Lord has not appeared to you" (Exodus 4:1).* But the Lord responded by empowering him with the ability to perform miraculous signs. But Moses was not satisfied; yet again, he responded, *O my Lord, I am not eloquent... I am slow of speech and slow of tongue (Exodus 4:10).* Yet, God assured him that He would be with his mouth (Exodus 4:12). Still unwilling to heed God's call and rather concerned about his weakness, Moses said, *O my Lord, please send by the hand of whomever else You may send (Exodus 4:13).* Still, the Lord would use no one else, but Moses.

Despite his initial unwillingness, fear, and his clear

inabilities, Moses' eventual successes is clear proof that grace is what makes the difference. If Moses trusted in anything, it surely couldn't have been his leadership skills or oratory prowess. It had to have been the grace of God upon him to get the job done. He certainly wasn't confident in his own natural abilities. He understood that his own abilities would result in a fiasco.

Earlier on, when he attempted to save the Israelites in his own wisdom and abilities, he killed an Egyptian and got into trouble for it. It isn't hard to tell why he became so reluctant to yield God's calling to return to the same assignment. This is probably why God took a special interest in him and wouldn't send anyone else. Moses had learned, by experience, that his human strength would fail him. He had come to understand the fact that he wouldn't succeed, going by his human strength. Perhaps, this was the exact quality that God loved about him. No wonder it was said of him, *the man Moses was very humble, more than all the men that were on the face of the earth (Numbers 12:3).*

Moses' posture is just completely in sync with Paul's confessions: *...I will rather boast in my infirmities, that the power of Christ may rest upon me. Therefore, I will take pleasure in infirmities, in reproaches, in needs, in persecutions, in distresses, for Christ's sake. For when I am weak, then I am made strong (2 Corinthians 12:9-10).* Moses "took pleasure" in his weaknesses when he expressed the natural impossibilities of the task God was sending him to undertake as well as his physical limitations. Even though he was doing this to "discourage" God from using him, he was indirectly expressing his humility—the fact that he didn't trust in his own abilities. It isn't surprising that he went on to show unparalleled trust and confidence in God's power, later on. On several occasions, when it appeared as though the children of Israel were in trouble, with no way of escape, Moses showed an unusual trust in God's power. This always paid off, as God, through him, performed some of the most astounding miracles in the Bible.

Moses' story lets us see that confidence in God's grace is greater than our natural abilities and skills. However, this isn't to say that our abilities and natural advantages are useless. What is important is to understand that it is God's grace on these advantages that ends up producing lasting results. When we choose to be more confident of the grace of God on our lives than anything else, we'll be able to get the power of God to work through us when our natural abilities fail. Confidence in the grace of God means we understand that it is not by power nor might, but by God's spirit in us (Zechariah 4:6).

The Grace at Work in Us

In the secular world, we understand the need to ensure that anyone we entrust with a task is equipped with the necessary information, document, knowledge, and skills to execute the task successfully. If, in our human wisdom, we could be so meticulous, how much more God, the one who created us? We are all equipped with the grace to function effectively in whatever responsibility that God has committed to our trust. We have to be conscious of this to be able to walk continually in it.

Now, depending on the things we do and the specific direction of God for our lives, the grace of God equips us to do them effectively. However, since we aren't necessarily directed to do the same things in the same way, the grace of God equips us with different abilities. In other words, we may not, every single one of us may have the capacity to function better than others at specific things we do. The epistle to the Romans paints a clear picture of this:

For as we have many members in one body, but all members have not the same function, so we, being many, are one body in Christ, and individually members one of another. **Having then gifts differing according to the grace that is given to us**, *let us use them: if prophecy, let us prophesy in proportion to our faith; or ministry, let us use it in our ministering; he who teaches, in teaching; he who exhorts, in exhortation... (Romans 12:4-8).*

Here, the point is not to say we can't prophesy, teach, and exhort excellently if we choose to. As a matter of fact, we can. However, the point to note is the fact that whatever task or responsibility that God has entrusted to us comes with specific workings of God's grace in us which equips us with certain ennoblements or abilities. The apostle Peter refers to the same thing when he writes to the church, *as each one of you has received a gift, minister it to one another, as good stewards of the manifold grace of God (1 Peter 4:10).* Paul also has several instances when he speaks of the grace of God upon his life. Here are a few examples:

I have written more boldly to you on some points, as reminding you, because of **the grace given to me by God,** *that I might be a minister of Jesus Christ, ministering the gospel of God (Romans 15:15-16).*

According to the grace which was given to me, *as a wise master builder, I have laid the foundation and another builds on it (1 Corinthians 3:10).*

...of which I became a minister **according to the measure of the grace of God given to me** *by the effective working of His power. To me, who am less than the least of all the saints,* **this grace was given**, *that I should preach among the gentiles the unsearchable riches of Christ (Ephesians 3:7-8).*

Just as it was with the apostle Paul, the grace of God given to us works out certain unique abilities through each of us. As a result, we are at our best when we align ourselves to the specific things that God has equipped us to do. Over the years, I have remained true and focused on God's leading for me. This is where His grace and divine enablement in me find expression. I know several other women who have changed the lives of many people around the world, simply by staying true to the desires and things that God had deposited in them. Like myself, many of these women, going by their temperaments or natural make-ups, couldn't have been able to do the things that they do. It has to be a function of the grace of God upon their lives!

Why Is It Called "Grace?"

You may just have wondered why Scriptures use the term, "grace," is used in reference to the divine ennoblements of God in us. Well, the reason is not far-fetched. The term is also commonly used in reference to the gospel of salvation, as that which is not merited by works, but found only in Christ. Here are a few relevant examples:

But none of these things moves me; nor do I count my life dear to myself so that I may finish my race with joy, and the ministry which I have received from the Lord Jesus, to testify to the gospel of the grace of God (Acts 20:24).

...Being justified freely by His grace through the redemption that is in Christ Jesus (Romans 3:24).

Therefore, having been justified by faith, we have peace with God through our Lord Jesus Christ, through whom we have access into this grace wherein we stand... (Romans 5:1-2).

For by grace, you have been saved through faith, and that not of yourselves; it is the gift of God, not of works, lest anyone should boast (Ephesians 2:8-9).

In the context of the above verses of Scripture, it is clear that "grace" is used to express the fact that something is free of charge and not worked for. This Amplified Bible makes this clearer. Acts 20:24, for instance, is rendered thus: ... *and the ministry which I received from the Lord Jesus, to testify of the good news of God's **[precious, undeserved] grace** [which makes us free of the guilt of sin and grants us eternal life].*

The distinctive quality of grace is the fact that it is undeserved and earned without labor. This is obviously true of our salvation in Christ. It is the same with our divine enablement and gifts as well. What this means is that we do not merit these abilities by our own selves. It is a function of God's liberal bestowment on our lives so that we can be able to bless others as well. No wonder our Lord Jesus Christ told His disciples: ... *freely* you have received, freely give (Matthew 10:8).*

Holding On by the Grace of God

If we have been supplied with all the enablement required to carry out the responsibilities that God has committed to us, then, we also have the ability to hold on. Holding on, in this context, refers to staying firm in God's will irrespective of temptations, trials, and challenges. This is obviously one of the divine abilities required to fulfill God's will for our lives successfully. When we walk in line with God's plans for us, we have the divine ability to absorb whatever challenge comes our way. The Lord expressed this very fact to Paul when He told him, *My grace is sufficient for you, for My strength is made perfect in weakness (2 Corinthians 12:9).* Now, the following verses show us that Paul's weaknesses included external challenges like persecutions, reproaches, needs, distresses, etc. Yet, God's grace was sufficient enough to help him hold on through such periods.

Humility Is Trusting in the Grace of God

I am quite certain that one of the key reasons (if not the single reason) why Moses was described as a very humble man is because of his dependency on God. This was a man who knew he had very little to offer relative to the task God wanted to be accomplished. Such a mindset was all he needed, and that was all that God wanted from him. God is only able to use people who are totally yielded and submitted to Him. *...But on this one will I look: On him who is poor and of a contrite spirit, and one who trembles at My word (Isaiah 66:2).* This was exactly what Moses was.

We live in a world that places so much emphasis on our own physical abilities. We are quite familiar with motivational clichés that only tell us about the power of the self. Even though these clichés help to inspire and stir us to strive to be the best we can, they aren't necessarily sufficient in dealing with some of the serious challenges we face. Most importantly, such clichés aren't exactly relevant to us when we choose to serve God, irrespective of what we feel or experience. This is because our desire to serve God and do

His will is, in itself, a disregard of our own selves. It is about submitting to God's abilities, rather than ours. Hence, the moment we are focused on our own abilities, we can tell that we aren't submitting to the will of God.

Submission to God entails submission to His word, His will and His power for our lives. This means there is very little room to depend on our own abilities. This is what it means to trust and submit to His grace. In other words, when we trust in our abilities, we only get the best they can offer. However, when we submit to God, we give room for His power to be expressed through us. Just like Paul, we have to boast in our infirmities and take pleasure in our limitations, if we want the power of Christ may rest upon us. This means our weaknesses is all we should boast about if at all we need to boast about anything. Like the apostle, we have to be conscious of the fact that we are made strong, only when we are weak (2 Corinthians 12:10).

Often times, when we think about humility, we think in terms of human relationships with one another. We fail to consider the fact that true humility is submission to the grace of God. Our submission to the gospel, which is the grace of God in Christ, is what got us saved in the first place. We earned salvation freely, without contributing anything or meriting it by our own abilities (Ephesians 2:8-9). In the same vein, it is our submission to His grace that determines how effectively we walk in His will and how successful we become while living for Him. The Lord Jesus helps us understand why this is so with his parable of two men, a Pharisee (a religious scholar) and a tax collector (who was seen as a sinner) who went to the temple to pray:

The Pharisee stood and prayed thus with himself, God, I thank You that I am not like other men —extortioners, unjust, adulterers, or even as this task collector. I fast twice a week; I give tithe of all that I possess. And the tax collector, standing afar off, would not so much as raise his eyes to heaven, but beat his breast saying, God, be merciful to me a sinner (Luke 18:11-13)

Going by our natural feelings, we would prefer the Pharisee to the tax collector. We see the Pharisee as a meticulous, detailed, and serious-minded fellow, who was confident in his ability. We've been wired by the society to believe such persons are the best we can have around us. On the other hand, we see the tax collector as a weak person and a failure. However, the Lord is of a different opinion. He says that the tax collector goes home justified, rather than the Pharisee. In His words, *everyone who exalts himself will be humbled, and he who humbles himself will be exalted (Luke 18:14)*.

Jesus cared more about the extent of their submission to God. The Pharisee trusted in himself, while the tax-collector trusted in God's ability. Well, it appears the Pharisee had clear reasons to trust in his abilities. However, Jesus refers to such as pride. Disregarding our own abilities, exalting God's power at work in us is the true humility.

…Therefore He says: "God resists the proud, but gives more

grace to the humble." Therefore submit to God… Humble yourselves in the sight of the Lord, and He will lift you up (James 4:6-7, 10)

How to Submit to Grace

Realizing that true humility entails submission to God's power and ability at work in us surely is important. However, knowing exactly how to submit ourselves is a lot more important. Of course, a mindset that is in submission to God surely culminates in corresponding actions and decisions. Hence, we surely have to begin with the right mindset. I have identified two major ways through which we can practically submit to grace always.

<u>Through prayers and study</u>: Apparently, these two factors reverberate through all aspects of our Christian experience. They certainly determine the quality of our spiritual lives, our fellowship with God, our desires, etc. Much more than these, they are expressions of our submission to God. When we pray, it is an expression of our dependence on God's power. Prayer is an apt way of showing and demonstrating that we do not depend on our own abilities or ideas, but God's. Hence, the extent to which we give ourselves to prayers is the extent to which we express our unwavering trust in God's grace. Similarly, giving ourselves to fellowshipping with God's word means we believe that our human wisdom or knowledge is insufficient.

<u>Giving glory to God</u>: The Bible declares that Abraham *did not waver at the promise of God through unbelief, but was strengthened in faith*, **giving glory to God** *(Romans 4:20)*. What this means is that Abraham constantly demonstrated the fact that God's power holds sway in his life. This must have been evident in his words and actions. When we give glory to God, we take our own natural abilities out of the spotlight. Instead, we choose to let others know that our dependency and trust is on God.

Just like the Pharisee in Jesus' story, we tend, as humans, to emphasize our own "glory" and boast about the things we have done or can do. However, Jesus lets us know that anyone who exalts himself is humbled, and anyone who humbles himself is exalted (Luke 18:14). We humble ourselves by simply demonstrating that all we are is by God's grace, with our words and actions. Paul did just this, in his epistle to the Corinthians: *but by the grace of God I am what I am (1 Corinthians 15:10)*. We can do the same before all persons we encounter.

God has equipped us with the grace and enablement to execute and hold on to His will. However, we are only able to walk in sync with this grace when we submit our natural ideas and abilities for God's. This is demonstrated by our continual fellowship with Him and our emphasis on His power instead of ours.

Prayer

Dear Father, I thank You for the stupendous grace which You have bestowed on me. I choose to be humble. I choose to trust in Your grace and abilities at work in me, instead of mine. I refuse to be full of myself. I choose to give You all the glory in my words and actions, in Jesus' name. Amen!

A Glance through Your Bible

2 Corinthians 12:7-10; 2 Timothy 2:1-3

2 Corinthians 12:7 And lest I should be exalted above measure by the abundance of revelation that is given to me, a messenger of Satan to buffet me, lest I be exalted above measure. 8Concerning this thing I pleaded with the Lord three times that it might depart from me. 9And He said to me, "My grace is sufficient for you, for my strength is made perfect in weakness." 10Therefore, most gladly, I will rather boast in my infirmities, that the power of Christ may rest upon me. Therefore, I will take pleasure in infirmities, in reproaches, in needs, in persecutions, in distresses, for Christ's sake. For when I am weak, then I am made strong.

____

____

2 Timothy 2:1 You therefore my son, be strong in the grace that is in Christ Jesus. 2And the things that you have heard from me among many witnesses, commit these to faithful

men who will be able to teach others also. ³You must endure hardship as a good soldier of Jesus Christ.

Study Questions

- What are the benefits of God's grace on our lives?
- Why is it important to trust in the grace of God more than our human abilities?
- What was that unique thing about Moses that made him express so much trust in God's power?
- The Scriptures describe the supernatural abilities of God on our lives as "grace." Why?
- What are the practical ways to submit to the grace of God on our lives?

Afterword

We Can Start Carrying Out Great Exploits Now!

…but the people who know their God shall be strong, and shall carry out great exploits (Daniel 11:32)

It is a fact that many societies of the world are wired to underrate the woman and to give her only little opportunities to thrive. However, the reality that we find in God's word lets us know that we can excel, make stupendous impacts, and do great exploits in the world, irrespective of any opposition. If we, as women, would choose to occupy our natural places of influence, we can constantly make indelible impacts in the world. This isn't difficult to see in the family setting, for instance. Throughout history, some of the most impactful people in the world were primarily shaped and influenced by their mothers. Such influence, when extended outside the family setting, can prove to be an invaluable means of causing a change in our world. Irrespective of the societal or cultural limitations around, we all have the natural grace to cause changes around us.

When women pray, much power is made available to cause changes in our lives around the world. Prayer is where it all starts. It is the foundational means of causing changes around us. Besides, it is also a means of fellowship with God. Such fellowship provides us with the opportunity to receive God's thoughts and ideas regarding our societies and the world around us. It also helps us maintain the zeal and grace to keep us through difficult times. It is through this fellowship in prayer that God's gifts in us are stirred-up for expression. Hence, we all have to begin in the place of prayer. You can start making impacts around you by giving yourself constantly to all kinds of intercession and supplication.

God uses those who care and are willing. We present ourselves as people who care about the situations around us when we make ourselves available in prayer to God. By praying for changes in our world, we can be equipped with the wherewithal to bring about those changes. It all begins with our submission to God in prayers!

The Bible tells us about the story of Nehemiah. Jerusalem's temple, walls, and gates had been long destroyed by Babylon. The people of Judah had all been scattered, with many taken into exile. When the news eventually came to Nehemiah, who was in Persia, his immediate response shows his palpable zeal and concern for the city: *so it was, when I heard these words, that I sat down and wept, and mourned for many days;*

I was fasting and praying before the God of heaven (Nehemiah 1:4). He was obviously touched and concerned; however, it is important to note that he didn't just mourn. He gave his concern an expression, by his fasting and prayer "before the God of heaven." While it is highly commendable that he was so concerned, his apt choice to prayer and fasting shows that he wasn't displaying vain emotions; he was prepared to cause a change. His trust in God's word, as well as his concern for the people and the city, was palpable in his prayers to God:

Remember, I pray, the word that You commanded Your servant Moses, saying, "if you are unfaithful, I will scatter you among the nations, but if you return to Me, and keep My commandments and do them, though some of you were cast out to the farthest part of the heavens, yet I will gather them from there, and bring them to the place which I have chosen as a dwelling for My name." Now, these are Your servants and Your people, whom You have redeemed by Your great power, and by Your strong hand. O Lord, I pray, please let Your ear be attentive to the prayer of Your servants who desire to fear Your name... (Nehemiah 1:8-11).

Nehemiah eventually got the approval and support of King Artaxerxes, to whom he was a cup bearer. Amazingly, the king also granted his request for letters and all necessary documents to aid with an easy passage to build the city, and for all the supplies required. Bible scholars argue that such generosity was quite unlikely of the king, as he was the one who had earlier ordered the initial work in the city to be stopped (Ezra 4:21-23). Besides, Nehemiah's request to leave serving him for something else wasn't something the king could have ideally taken lightly. It was clear that Nehemiah was divinely favored to carry out the rebuilding process. Eventually, his activities did not only result in the rebuilding of the city walls; the Jewish community in Jerusalem was restored, revived, and repopulated. It was a new dawn! But it all started with Nehemiah's genuine concern, which was aptly put into fasting and prayers.

Just like Nehemiah, we require a genuine concern and passion to make exploits and cause indelible changes in our world. It is normal and conventional to get emotional with the uninspiring news and happenings around us; however, true concern is demonstrated when we take the necessary actions towards birthing a change. Nehemiah fasted and prayed, with a genuine passion and a trust in the word of God. Similarly, we can give ourselves to praying for a change. Just like Mary (the mother of John Mark), Rhoda, and other members of the church took it upon themselves to pray for Peter's deliverance, rather than whining and complaining (Acts 12: 1-18), we also can express faith in the effectiveness of our prayers. We can do this by going to the place of prayers when we hope to cause a change.

Having prayed, Nehemiah got all the help he needed to physically address what he had thoroughly toiled and labored for in prayer. His actions eventually culminated in a total revival. What if he hadn't given himself to prayer? When we choose to go to God in prayer, as a first approach to addressing the things we are concerned about, we express our faith and trust in God's power, grace and ability. To do otherwise would be an expression of pride, a dependency on our own human strength, influence, skills, or abilities, which is surely insufficient. *...for by strength, no man shall prevail (1 Samuel 2:9); Not by power nor by might, but by My spirit, says the Lord of hosts (Zechariah 4:6).*

The apt response to the challenges around us is to go to God in prayers. When we do this, we express our faith and dependence on Him, thus taking custody of His power to cause changes around us. Having prayed, when we go about the required physical tasks and processes to addressing our challenges, it is easier to get the results we desire. Nehemiah got his request from King Artaxerxes to depart his presence and to go about building of the walls of the city of Jerusalem when it was naturally unlikely. He supernaturally got all required supports to accomplish this task. This obviously happened because he had prayed. The positive response and supports he got from the king were a clear demonstration of the power of God. Esther's story is also quite similar. She found favor of the king, to spare the lives of all the Jews when a date had already been fixed for their extermination. The deliverance of the whole Jews in the Persian Empire (Esther Chapter 4 & 5) would, most likely, not have happened if she hadn't given herself to fasting and prayer before she met with the king.

Another very noticeable fact from Nehemiah's story is the

fact that he truly loved the people. His concern apparently wasn't just about the walls of the city or the temple that was destroyed. More importantly, he felt compassion for the people of Judah who had been scattered about in exile. He surely was planning to rebuild the city so that the Jewish people could return home so that the community can be revived again. His prayers to God show that he was more concerned for the people than just some inanimate walls: *please let Your ear be attentive and Your eyes open that You may hear the prayer of Your servant which I pray before You now, day and night,* **for the children of Israel, Your servants** *(Nehemiah 1:6).*

Like Nehemiah, our prayers, actions, etc. shouldn't be about our selfish desires, but something born out of a genuine concern for the people around us. True exploits begin with prayers, but not just any prayer; it begins with prayers born out of genuine passion for the people. Our exploits wouldn't be about us, our personal achievements or pursuits. They would be about how much we have contributed and added to others.

The Lord Jesus Christ gave us a picture of what it means to do exploits in the world around us: *As the Father has sent Me, I also send you (John 20:21).* His words elsewhere help make the picture clearer, expressing what exactly He has sent us to do: *...but whosoever will be great among, let him be your servant. And whoever desires to be first among you, let him be your slave—just as the Son of Man did not come to be served,* *but to serve, and to give His life a ransom for many (Matthew 20:26-28)*. True exploits entail a life that is spent in service to others and not one that is lived caring only for ourselves, people, and things that are immediately connected to us. Our core activities, projects, desires, should be to serve others. Jesus lets us see that true greatness is found in this. Living a life of great exploits by serving others surely doesn't entail neglecting our loved ones or our well-being. However, like Jesus, we should live with the consciousness of the genuine needs of others.

God's will is for us is to represent Him on earth, irrespective of gender, race or status; we are all one in Christ (Galatians 3:28). Hence, as women, we have a right to put ourselves in places of influence, to live for the benefit of others, in whatever capacity we can. When we pray, power is made available to cause changes in our world. In addition to this, God has equipped us with inherent gifts by His grace, with which we can impact the world around us, functioning in different positions and capacities. However, we have to respond to these advantages by putting ourselves in the right position for us—in places of influence. We can begin to do exploits even now, with those closest to us.

What is important for us to note is the fact that influence begins with a genuine concern for others, and a prompt response in the place of prayers. When we pray, we place a demand on God's supernatural power. Thus, He hears us and answers our prayers. When we pray with a genuine passion for a change or a divine influence in the lives of those around us, He answers our prayers. Often times, He does so by equipping us with the ideas, skills, and competencies to bring about such changes. So much happens when we pray and get into fellowship with God; it is the place of our strength and capacity to do exploits!

www.ingramcontent.com/pod-product-compliance
Lightning Source LLC
Chambersburg PA
CBHW031124130726
47988CB00006B/2212